NEW YORK REVIEW BOOKS
CLASSICS

W9-ASZ-830

PEKING STORY

DAVID KIDD (1926–1996) was born in Corbin, Kentucky to
a coal-mining community. He later grew up in Detroit, where
his father became an executive in the automotive industry. In
1946, at age 19, Kidd made his first trip to Peking as a University of Michigan exchange student with one idea in mind:
to get as far away from home as possible. He spent the next
four years teaching English in the Peking suburbs. During this
time, he married the daughter of a former Chief Justice of the
Supreme Court, moving into her family's 101-room palace,
where he had a uniquely intimate view of the Communist
takeover. His account of his experiences was serialized in *The
New Yorker* and published in book-form as *All the Emperor's
Horses* in 1960, later retitled *Peking Story: The Last Days of
Old China*. He returned to the US in 1950 and taught at the
Asia Institute until 1956, when he moved to Japan. There he
continued to work as a lecturer, became a devoted collector of
Chinese and Japanese art and antiquities, and, in 1976, founded
the Oomoto School of Traditional Japanese Arts in Kyoto. He
lived in Kyoto until his death of cancer at age 69.

JOHN LANCHESTER is the prize-winning author of the novels
Fragrant Harbour, *The Debt to Pleasure*, and *Mr. Phillips*.
Brought up in Hong Kong, where his family had lived since
the 1930s, he now lives in London with his wife and son.

PEKING STORY

THE LAST DAYS OF OLD CHINA

DAVID KIDD

Preface by
JOHN LANCHESTER

NEW YORK REVIEW BOOKS

New York

This is a New York Review Book
Published by The New York Review of Books
1755 Broadway, New York, NY 10019

Grateful acknowledgment is given for the use of the following photographs: the
views of the interior of the Summer Palace, from the collection of Adrian Evans,
1948; the Summer Palace in winter, from the collection of Glenn Shaw, 1913.

Nine of the stories in this book were previously published individually in *The
New Yorker* and in a book entitled *All the Emperor's Horses* by David Kidd. A
portion of "Return to Peking" first appeared in *Connoisseur*.

Library of Congress Cataloging-in-Publication Data
Kidd, David.
  Peking story : the last days of old China / David Kidd : preface by
John Lanchester.
      p. cm. — (New York review books classics)
  ISBN 1-59017-040-7 (pbk. : alk. paper)
  1. China—Social life and customs—1949-1976. 2. Communism—China.
I. Title. II. Series.
  DS777.6.K53 2003
  951.05—dc21

                          2003011656

ISBN 1-59017-040-7

Book design by Lizzie Scott
Printed in the United States of America on acid-free paper.
10 9 8 7 6 5 4 3 2 1

June 2003
www.nyrb.com

THIS BOOK IS DEDICATED TO
THE MEMORY OF MY PATRON,

DR. JOHN LEIGHTON STUART,

THE AMERICAN AMBASSADOR TO CHINA
FROM 1946 TO 1949

CONTENTS

PREFACE

CHINA LIVED through three revolutions in the 20th century: the revolution which displaced the Emperor and replaced him with elected government, in 1911; the Communist revolution, which took place in 1949, with Mao Tse-Tung's victory in the Civil War; and the Cultural Revolution, which began in the mid-1960s. *Peking Story* is a beautiful and deceptively simple book set at the midpoint of these three great convulsions. David Kidd, a young American student of Chinese on an exchange program, arrived in Peking in 1948, just as the Communists were completing their victory in the Civil War, and he left it two years later, as the regime's oppressive nature was beginning to be more fully manifested. *Peking Story* belongs to the kind of art which tells a large story by concentrating on a small one. It is the story of one of the century's great disasters, a book which, by its lightness of touch and careful selection of detail, manages to tell the reader a lot about what happened to China in the 20th century, and the extent of the human and cultural losses involved.

Kidd's narrative is not panoramic. He concentrates on the story of the Yu family, into which he married just as Peking was falling to the Communists, and just as the family patriarch was dying. Old Mr. Yu had been the Chief Justice of China, a job of almost unimaginable grandeur. The wealth and importance of the Yus is sketched in a couple of *Peking*

Story's many telling asides. The judge had once traded "a country estate in the Western Hills"—note the singular indefinite article—for a pair of antique porcelain cups. Elsewhere Kidd mentions a friend of the family whose sister "should have been the last empress of China," if she had not been "passed over because of a slight mental disorder and having one leg shorter than the other."

Most of all, though, the power and glamour of the Yu family is concentrated in their house. It is not quite clear—though it is a bit clearer than Kidd might have wanted it to be—whether he fell in love with his wife Aimee, the fourth of nine Yu daughters, or with the Yu palace, with its high walls and huge traditional garden, its Pavilion of Harmonious Virtues, Hall of Ancient Pines, beams of ancient cedar, and tiles which "rivaled in blackness and smoothness those of the Imperial Palace." The life of an ancien régime never seems as sweet as in the last moments before its collapse, and the life of the Yus in their home seems very sweet indeed—calm, beautiful, orderly, all these qualities intensified by the fact that this old life is doomed.

Kidd does not waste any time pretending to be even-handed about the Communists. Right at the beginning of the book we are told of trouble with the family servants, who "under the influence of the Communists . . . grew insolent and lazy. Fires were made carelessly or not at all, and meals were late and unappetizing." China was a horribly unequal society, and this fact made many observers and many more Chinese entertain hopes that the Communists might be less bad than their Kuomintang predecessors; even people with few illusions thought that they might be less corrupt. These hopes made some people slow to see the realities of life in New China. Not Kidd. The Yus were so privileged that they had no on-the-one-hand, on-the-other-hand ambivalence about the Communists: the family had nowhere to go but down. This helped them, and Kidd, to see the new regime more clearly than people who had, or hoped that they might have, something to gain.

The story of the Yu family is sad, but *Peking Story* is not a depressing book, because Kidd's eye for comedy and his sense of detail makes it bright with life. In later years Kidd did not write fiction—his many books were about aspects of Japanese culture and aesthetics—but his eye for character was such that he could have. The Yu family are sketched quickly but vividly: Aimee, his wife, quick and tough, never taking a backward step in confrontations with the authorities; Aunt Chin, who "kept cats, had asthma, and seldom left the house, or even her own rooms," but is nonetheless shrewd, generous, and devastatingly good at cards. The outsiders are vivid too, like the shabby Reverend Mr. Feng with his astonishingly loud voice, and the half-mad chef Lao Pei, who "sometimes banged his head against the rockery in my garden until blood dripped from his hair. He was overwhelmed, he explained, by the woes of China." This is something of a theme in *Peking Story*. He attends a play that is interrupted by young Communists so carried away by the production that they begin to suffer from fits, foaming at the mouth and passing into convulsions. The scene is Dostoevskian in its combination of comedy and horror, and also in its view of revolutionary fervor as a madness. Kidd could be dry about the revolution—the play stars a vicious old hag "who was a personification, it was made clear to us, of *some* of the evils of the old capitalistic society"—but at heart he saw it as a form of insanity.

This is not to say that Kidd's aesthetics were Dostoevskian; on the contrary. He was an aesthete and an exquisite, and photographs of the author make it clear that he was no mean work of art himself. He was a great noticer of clothes. These provide a running theme in *Peking Story*. It is typical that when recounting his first meeting with Aimee, the first (and main) thing he notices are her clothes: she wore "a tight, high-collared, white silk dress, slit to the thighs, and carried an ivory fan in her hand on which shone a green jade ring." The lavish clothes of old rich China are in striking contrast with the new puritanism of the Communists; a motif that carries on through the "sky-blue gown of fine Tibetan felt, and a vestlike jacket of patterned silk" that Kidd wears on his wedding day, to the riot of costumes at the final party in the Yu garden (especially the "Mongolian princess, complete with oiled black hair encrusted with coral and turquoise, and arranged over a frame of what looked like horns," and who turns out in fact to be a Mongolian prince), to the night when Kidd is finally arrested and goes to the police station in "an enormous blue-brocaded dressing gown that had been worn at the imperial court by one of [Aimee's] ancestors. It expressed my feelings towards the People's Soldiers at that moment. If I could have found the sable hat topped with peacock feathers that went with it, I might have put that on, too."

Kidd was deeply in love with the material culture of old China. One of the most heartfelt passages in *Peking Story* concerns Justice Yu's old incense braziers, whose extraordinary colors are kept alive by fires that must never be allowed to go out—fires which, in the case of these particular braziers, "glowing and shimmering like jewels, no two alike," have been burning for five hundred years. A vengeful servant girl deliberately extinguishes the braziers, whose beauty can never be recaptured. It says a lot for Kidd's art that this act of spite towards a set of objects can seem so horribly cruel, and such a portent for China's future.

Kidd was not quite twenty when he went to Peking, and only twenty-four when he left in 1950. *Peking Story* is the story of a young man written by an older one, which is part of why it is simultaneously so vivid, so simple, so calm, and so sad. The magnificent last chapter of the book carries the story of the Yu family, and of David and Aimee, up to 1981.

Without wanting to give too much away, I think it is clear that Peking was the shaping event of Kidd's life. After getting in trouble in McCarthyite America—his years in Communist China making him automatically an object of suspicion—Kidd went to live in Japan, where he eventually founded the Oomoto School of the Traditional Arts in Kyoto. The school taught the arts associated with the tea ceremony, pottery, aikido, and the Noh theatre. Kidd had seen one traditional culture destroyed deliberately, and so he dedicated his life to preventing another one from being killed by neglect. His Kyoto house, Togendo, was a famous masterpiece of calm and order and traditional aesthetics. He died in 1996.

—JOHN LANCHESTER

INTRODUCTION

PEKING was my home from 1946 to 1950, two years before the Communist revolution and two years after. As the American half of an exchange between the University of Michigan, where I was a student of Chinese culture, and Peking's Yenching University, I left for China immediately after graduation, arriving at Peking in the autumn of 1946, still two months short of my twentieth birthday.

Peking was everything I expected it to be—a great walled and moated medieval city enclosing some one million people in twenty-five square miles of palaces, mansions, gardens, shops, and temples, the center of what once had been the world's largest empire. I never met anyone who did not fall in love with the city, if not at first sight, at least after the first week. I could even speak some Chinese, thanks to the valiant efforts of Mr. T'ien, my Chinese teacher at Michigan.

Peking's immense outer walls were pierced by sixteen towered double gates, while at its heart another set of moats and walls enclosed the imperial palace, known as the Purple Forbidden City. This city-within-a-city had been the unmoving purple polestar, the heaven-and-earth-touching vertical axis, around which the whole earth turned. Seated in state on his elevated throne in the main hall of this vast complex of buildings, the emperor faced due south along the central horizontal axis of the city, arched over by a series of monumental gates, the sacrosanct meridian through which imperial power reached out to all of China and, from there, the world.

I could not have guessed during those early months that I would experience the last siege of the greatest walled city in the world or that I would marry into an old and aristocratic Peking family. Instead, I blissfully went about the business of sightseeing and making friends, first with my Chinese colleagues at Yenching University, where I studied Chinese poetry, and at nearby Tsinghwa University, where I taught English. Later, I began to make friends with that extraordinary group of international foreigners for whom Peking was home. The city invited us to stay, to settle down in a fine old house, to enjoy its cedar-shaded courtyards, to give parties to view the moon or gardens filled with snow. Peking had the power to touch, transform, and refine all those who lived within its ancient walls.

Only a few Westerners who once lived there are still alive today—no more than ten or twenty of us at most, scattered throughout the world. I used to hope that some bright young scholar on a research grant would write about us and our Chinese friends before it was too late and we were all dead and gone, folding back into darkness the wonder that had been our lives.

To this day, no such scholar has appeared, leaving me, as far as I know, the lone, first-hand chronicler of those extraordinary years that saw the end of old China, and the beginning of the new.

—DAVID KIDD
Kujoyama, Kyoto

PEKING STORY

DRAGONS, PINK BABIES,
AND THE CONSULAR SERVICE

LATE IN January of 1949, Peking surrendered gracefully to the ever victorious Communist Army, and one day soon after, my fiancée—a Chinese girl—telephoned me to say that her father, who had been ill for a long while, was dying. We must marry immediately, Aimee said, or face the prospect of waiting out at least a year of mourning, as Chinese custom demanded. It seemed unfeeling to hold a wedding at such a time, and there was no way of guessing what the Communist authorities would say to a marriage between the daughter of a "bureaucratic-capitalist" Chinese and an American teacher, but the future was so uncertain that we decided we must go ahead. Aimee's family, when consulted, agreed. However, since we could not be sure we were not bringing some sort of trouble on them, we planned to keep the marriage a secret, at least for a while.

I had first met Aimee a year earlier one hot summer evening at a Peking opera theater in the South City. I had rented an open booth at the balcony railing where, in the heat, I indulged myself in the usual Chinese opera fan's pastime of cracking salted watermelon seeds between my teeth and drinking cup after cup of tea from the pot, replenished from time to time by the waiters, on my table. I noticed that the booth to my left was still unoccupied, but knew that many opera buffs never arrived until after ten, when the best actors appeared. Tonight Hsiao Ts'ui-hua, an impersonator of co-quettish girls, would end the program. He was one of the last actors in China who could still perform in toe shoes, the better to emulate the bound feet and swaying gait of a high-caste woman.

A drama had just ended and a placard announcing Mr. Hsiao as the last performer was already up when waiters began affixing red silk chair-backs and laying out teapots and cups in the next booth. At the same moment, a sudden murmur in the audience caused me to look toward the end of the aisle. Flanked by two maids in pale blue, Aimee stood in a doorway between curtains that had just been parted. She wore a tight, high-collared, white silk dress, slit to the thighs, and carried an ivory fan in her hand on which shone a green jade ring. She looked overwhelmingly cool and beautiful in that hot, smoke-filled theater. If more were needed, the elab-orate care with which the waiters ushered her to the booth next to mine was proof enough that she was a lady of distinc-tion. As she seated herself, I noticed the tip of a white jade pin in her hair and detected the faint but refreshing scent of sandalwood and jasmine.

The performance was about to begin, and I beckoned to a waiter indicating that I wished another pot of tea. When he approached, Aimee stopped him and spoke quickly in Chinese. After he left, she turned to me and said in much slower Chinese, "The tea here is too poor. I have asked him to prepare for you the tea I brought from home." Then she said in English, "It is only an ordinary tea, but I hope you will like it." I mumbled my thanks in both English and Chinese.

In due course the last opera, a comedy, began with Mr. Hsiao sailing across the stage, swaying gracefully on his famous, fluttering feet. The tea, when it came, was delicious. During the performance, Aimee and I, more often than not, laughed at the same time. I almost felt that I had come to the theater with her and wondered if she might be feeling the same. In any event, after the drama came to an end and Hsiao Ts'ui-hua had disappeared from the stage for good, Aimee introduced herself and asked, in careful Chinese again, if I cared to visit backstage and meet Mr. Hsiao. I accepted with pleasure.

We found the actor in his dressing room before a mirror, removing his makeup with cold cream. Meanwhile attendants were busy, first removing the rows of glittering colored stones from his black wig, next the wig and its many separate pieces, and last the bands of starched white cotton placed at the hairline which, Aimee explained to me, when applied wet, tightened the actor's face, creating the illusion of youth I had seen on stage. Seated before me now, his makeup, jewels, and starched bands removed, Mr. Hsiao was an old and ordinary looking man. Amused at my surprise, Aimee wrote out her address and invited me to tea a few days later, where I learned that she could play the violin, had studied gypsy dancing—complete with tambourine—from White Russians in Peking, knew classical Chinese dance, and, to my surprise, had majored in chemistry at the university. I also discovered that she was the fourth daughter of the former Chief Justice of the Chinese Supreme Court.

I was to meet Aimee's father only once. (Her mother was dead.) Even then, dressed in a padded blue silk gown and wearing a black silk cap, the elegant old man looked frail and ill, his skin appearing almost translucent. He received me in a building in the Yu mansion called the Eastern Study where he was occupied, at the time, in examining a pair of rare porcelain stem cups. When he let me handle them, I felt immensely honored. Now he lay on his death bed.

Thus began the events that led to the unseemly haste of our wedding.

Peking had, of course, just been through a siege of over a month. I had been cut off from the National Tsinghwa

University, some six miles outside the city, where I taught English, and had been living in a small house in Peking that I had previously rented for use on weekends and holidays. I liked the address—Bean Curd Puddle Lane. During the siege, Aimee used to bring me tureens of fatty pork cooked with aniseed, and invite me to unbelievable banquets for two in her family's enormous house. Her source of supply was a secret, and I had never asked her about it; I only knew that without her, and it, I would have had little besides watered rice to eat.

Now, though the siege was over, foreigners were forbidden to leave the city, so I was still unable to get back to my classes. Communist troops were quartered in the front court-yards of Aimee's home, and their horses were tethered in the garden, where they ate venerable and valuable chrysanthe-mum roots and became as much the subject of the family's complaints as the soldiers themselves. The family—Aimee's two brothers and eight sisters, plus wives, husbands, chil-dren, aunts, and uncles, about twenty-five people in all—spent most of its time complaining. The Communists were using a relatively light hand at the moment, but the men in the buildings around the front courtyards were taking up space, using precious water and electricity, and causing un-rest among the servants.

Aimee's people had lived in the old mansion for genera-tions. Surrounded, along with its outbuildings and its large garden, which must have been close to fifty thousand square feet in area, by a wall, it contained more than a hundred rooms, as well as a labyrinth of corridors and courts. It sprawled over several acres, and all the rooms were at one time warmed by radiant heat—that is, by charcoal fires kept burning under the tile floors—but after the revolution of 1911 the cost had become too great and coal stoves were installed. Although normally there were at least twenty servants, at the time of the siege there were fewer than ten, and after-ward, under the influence of the Communists, these grew insolent and lazy. Fires were made carelessly or not at all, and meals were late and unappetizing. One servant, laying a fire in the old man's sickroom, was heard telling the invalid—even then too ill to speak—that it was only a matter of time before they would see who would make whose fires. The servant was discharged, and spent the next two days wailing at the main gate, arousing deep sympathy among the soldiers. They were already suspicious of people living in so large a house, and now they became so surly and sullen that the family stopped using the main gate, coming and going instead by a small one that opened on a back alley. All in all, the situation was far from propitious for a wedding.

Some time before matters were brought to a head in this way, I had inquired at the American consulate about making my prospective marriage to a Chinese lawful in America. In essence, a Chinese marriage is simple. Two families make out a certificate, a number of friends witness the document in the presence of a respected friend of the two families, and that's all there is to it. Although divorce is rare, it is even easier. Both families simply agree to tear up the certificate. Nothing is made a matter of official record; the certificate form—a paper bordered with pictures of writhing pink babies and strings of gold coins—can be bought at any stationer's and filled in by the parties concerned.

The American government, I was told at the consulate, looks upon a Chinese wedding—which is a civil and personal, but not a religious, ceremony—as scarcely a matrimonial bond at all, recognizing a marriage with a Chinese only when it is recorded in sacred archives, after a ceremony conducted by someone of religious authority. The consulate also insisted that it must have a representative at the ceremony—although I am told this is not a State Department regulation—and that the consulate be paid a marriage-registration fee of one dollar.

When Aimee and I began hastily making our plans, her family said that they wanted whatever ceremony we had to be Chinese. Though religion has no part in a Chinese wedding, Aimee and I were sure we could persuade a Buddhist priest to preside at the ceremony, acting in place of the family friend and thus satisfying both the family and the consulate. This would be perhaps the first Chinese Buddhist wedding in history, and we were rather excited about it.

A day or two after I had informed the consulate of our intentions, a vice-consul named Kepler telephoned me to say that a Buddhist wedding wouldn't be legal in the eyes of the American government, any more than, say, a Taoist or Moslem wedding. Apparently these were all considered fly-by-night, unreliable religions, and the consulate, without quite saying so, excluded all but Christian ceremonies from their sanction. There was evidently nothing for it but to try to have a Christian ceremony that would seem as Chinese as possible. Mr. Kepler said he would see what he could do about finding us a Christian priest or minister, and I went to Aimee's house in the hope of breaking the news diplomatically.

Two days later, Mr. Kepler called me again. The Anglicans, the Methodists, the Presbyterians, and the Salvation Army had all been sounded out, and none of them was willing to give an interracial marriage its blessing without written consent from the parents of both bride and groom. I had received no mail from abroad since before the siege. I was not sure that letters were getting to America even yet, and it was unlikely that my mother would give her consent. Anyway, I couldn't write to her and get a reply in time.

I went to the consulate to canvass the possibility of being married in two ceremonies—a Chinese one immediately, and a Christian one when it could be arranged, for the benefit of the consulate and the sake of American legality. While I was discussing all this with Mr. Kepler, a Chinese porter, who was waxing the hall floor, stopped at the open office door. He introduced himself hesitantly and said perhaps he could help. "My brother is a Christian minister," he told us.

"Well, now, really?" said Mr. Kepler. "I didn't know that. What denomination? What is the name of his church?"

The porter said he didn't know, because he wasn't a Christian himself, and didn't particularly like his brother. But after all, he said, a brother is a brother, and if he could direct a little business his way, that was only proper. I asked him to send his brother to Aimee's house that evening, and said she and I would meet him there.

The minister came at seven o'clock. Aimee and I talked to him in a building called the Hall of Ancient Pines, which was in the garden and had been the favorite retreat of Aimee's father. It had become our own retreat from the endless complaints and histrionics of the rest of the family, which was feeling the uncertainties of a swiftly changing society, and especially the strain of playing host to the squatter troops in their house. "I am Reverend Joseph Feng," the minister told us. We soon discovered that this was all he could say in English. Even his Mandarin was poor, thickened by a heavy Cantonese accent, and Aimee had almost as much trouble understanding him as I did. He was the first Christian minister ever to set foot in that house. He was wearing a tattered brown tweed topcoat and pearl-gray spats, and, twisted about his neck, its ends hanging elegantly front and back, a once white silk scarf. He carried a carved cane, which, when he had sat down, he kept clutched between his knees. Aimee asked what denomination he belonged to, and he produced a worn piece of paper on which was written, above many seals and signatures, "Reverend Joseph Feng is an ordained clergyman of the Assemblies of God."

I had never heard of the Assemblies of God, but we were not inclined to question him too closely, being more than happy to accept him if the American consulate was satisfied. We knew that Aimee's family was indifferent to the religious aspects of the occasion, and was concerned only that the simple Chinese ceremony be included. As I have said, the signing of the certificate is the core of it; beyond that, there may be some slight additional ceremony, though this is not necessary. Both bride and bridegroom are sponsored by a relative or close friend, rings are exchanged, and the presiding friend—in this case the Reverend Mr. Feng—wishes the couple long life and many babies.

The Reverend Mr. Feng, probably briefed by his brother, quickly understood what was wanted, and I made an appointment to meet him in Mr. Kepler's office the next morning.

"Yes, yes," said Mr. Kepler when, with Mr. Feng beside me, I explained that we had found a suitable minister. "The Assemblies of God. That's fine! Fine! And when will the wedding be? I'm attending as the consular witness, you know."

Trying not to show the relief I felt, I told him the wedding would take place at Aimee's house two days later, at eight o'clock in the evening. I then explained that we were trying to keep our marriage a secret, particularly from the troops occupying the front courtyards of the house, since we didn't know what the reaction of the Communist authorities would be, and that we would tell anyone who might be curious about people coming and going that night that we were having a small private party. For some reason, the secrecy seemed to appeal to Mr. Kepler, and he said heartily, "You can depend on me!"

I pointed out that the Reverend Mr. Feng knew no English and that therefore the marriage ceremony would be entirely in Chinese. Mr. Kepler was sympathetic; he appeared to believe that conducting the Christian ceremony in Chinese had something to do with keeping the wedding a secret.

The Reverend Mr. Feng returned with me to Aimee's, where she and I spent some time haggling with him about his fee. There were many paper currencies in use in Peking then, and the stability of all of them was doubtful. When people discussed the price of anything more valuable than a pack of cigarettes, they talked in terms of silver or gold dollars, or perhaps pounds of millet or bolts of cloth. The Reverend Mr. Feng wanted silver—twenty Mexican dollars' worth. Five dollars Mex. would have paid a servant's wages for a month. We finally agreed on nine dollars Mex. It was high, but the Reverend—again, no doubt, briefed by his brother—was well aware of his value to us. We told him we were trying to keep the wedding as simple and as Chinese as possible, and asked for his cooperation. He promised to do his best.

Aimee and I had two days to get ourselves ready. Since I had no ring to give her, and no money to buy one, she gave me a diamond ring to put on her finger during the ceremony. I was not allowed to see her costume before the wedding, but she had already prepared mine—a sky-blue gown of fine Tibetan felt, and a vestlike jacket of patterned black silk to be worn over it. I was also to wear black silk shoes and white socks. Though details differ, this is a fairly standard formal wedding costume for men. Aimee didn't care for the garish red of the traditional Chinese wedding dress and would say only that she would wear a self-designed adaptation of it.

All the other details were left to friends and servants. I had been told not to appear before eight o'clock on the night of the wedding. It was decided to use the main gate again, for that night only; it was lacquered red and had a great, sweeping roof, and so would be much easier for our guests to find than the small one opening onto the back alley. There was an entrance court just inside the gate, and behind it lay the courtyards where the Communist soldiers were quartered.

The night of the wedding was cold, and when I arrived at the gate I found a group of soldiers warming themselves around a wood fire there. They seemed rather nervous and hostile—perhaps because of the sudden traffic that evening through the gate they had come to consider exclusively theirs. Off to the left, a little door in the wall of the entrance court opened on a corner of the garden, and I found a servant waiting beside the gate to lead the guests there. From inside the garden door, a line of paper lanterns hanging overhead marked out a way along stone and pebble paths, through rock grottoes, under a wisteria arbor, past faintly reeking, quietly chomping horses, through groves of rustling bamboo, to the Hall of Ancient Pines, where the wedding was to take place.

Ancient Pines was an imposing room, where many great men of China had been entertained by Aimee's father. Except for a few sofas and overstuffed chairs, it was furnished in Chinese style. The floors were of polished black tile and were covered with Chinese carpets. Six hexagonal lanterns of glass and carved wood hung in a row from the ceiling, and from the corners of each hung long red silk tassels. Potted flowering plants and orange and lime trees were scattered about the room, and Chinese landscape paintings decorated the walls, except for the north one, which was paneled with mirrors. When I arrived, about twenty guests were already there, and servants were carrying immense quantities of food and drink to various sideboards and tables. The windows had been covered with rice paper to shield us from the eyes of wandering soldiers.

Mr. Kepler was there, I saw, sitting directly under a lantern and talking, with visible enjoyment, to one of Aimee's attractive younger sisters. In a few minutes, Hetta Crouse, a mutual friend, came in with her husband, William Empson. Hetta is South African, and a sculptress; William is a British poet and critic, who was at that time teaching in Peking University. Hetta was to sponsor me, and I asked her if she had brought her seal.

I should explain that everyone in China has a seal. It is the equivalent of a signature, which is not valid there, the Chinese being convinced that a signature can easily be copied but that no two seals are ever alike. Even children have to use seals when they register in school or sign receipts for their supplies.

"I brought a whole bloody sackful," Hetta said, dumping a collection of seals of all sizes from her handbag onto a table. "Some of them are mine, and some are William's, and some are the ones the children use, and I don't know where we got the others. But we must use all of them on your certificate. They'll look *very* important."

In a short while, the Reverend Mr. Feng came in. He was dressed as before, with the dingy scarf hanging fore and aft, and his cane in hand. He carefully removed his coat, though not the scarf, switching the cane from one hand to the other as he did so, and, after shaking hands with me, joined Mr. Kepler. Servants continued to bring delicacies to the tables and sideboards until they could hold no more, and it became evident that both the food and the guests were ready. Then Mme. Hu, Aimee's godmother, who was to give her away, entered with a flourish and, speaking in English in deference to the foreigners present, announced, "The matrimony begins!"

The Reverend Mr. Feng jumped to his feet and, scarf flowing, strode to the center of the room just as Aimee appeared at the door, flanked by two of her sisters. Her dress, which went from neck to ankle, was scarlet, gold, and black. Enormous gold butterflies, and phoenixes dripping jewels and mounted on springs, trembled on her head. Coiled gold dragons hung from her ears. She was wearing the high-platformed shoes of the Manchu nobility, which had gone out of fashion more than a generation earlier, and, tottering into the room, she looked like something out of Chinese opera.

No one spoke. Aimee made her unsteady way to the side of the room opposite me, and immediately all the guests and participants except the Reverend Mr. Feng hurried to take their places with one or the other of us—Aimee's family and friends grouped behind her, and my party, which included Mr. Kepler but was decidedly outnumbered, behind me. Hetta stood at my elbow facing Mme. Hu and Aimee. The Reverend Mr. Feng was alone in the middle of the room, facing the south end, balancing himself lightly on his cane. After a moment, Aimee and I stepped in front of him, and I could see Aimee, her eyes demurely cast down, and the Reverend Mr. Feng's scarf reflected waveringly in the mellow old mirror panels of the north wall.

The Reverend Mr. Feng rolled his eyes upward and opened his mouth. No one was prepared for the volume of his voice. Aimee swayed visibly on her platforms. The reverberations of his first sentence faded, and he started again, softly, slowly, with agony in his voice, which increased in volume until he reached a new fortissimo. Again there was silence. We were steeling ourselves for a third outburst when he began a rhythmic chant that rose and fell. I was sure he had passed into a trance. Nothing he said was intelligible to me, but it certainly didn't sound like a marriage ceremony. Just what, I wondered, were the Assemblies of God, and what had we let ourselves in for?

I could see Hetta's frozen face in a corner of the mirror. I wondered what she was thinking—what they all were thinking. I hoped Mr. Kepler was satisfied with his Christian ceremony; this was all his fault. I looked directly at him, but his eyes were closed and his face expressionless. The food is cold, I thought. What can we do? Can't someone stop him?

I was suddenly aware that the Reverend Mr. Feng *had* stopped, and was looking at me. For a startled moment, I thought he had been reading my mind, and then I realized that I was missing a cue. I nodded my head slowly. I wasn't sure, but I supposed he had said the equivalent of "Do you take this woman..." He turned to Aimee and said something, and she nodded, too, so I knew I must have been right.

Aimee held out her left hand and I put the diamond ring on it; then I held out mine and she put an alexandrite ring on it. We bowed to the Reverend Mr. Feng, then to each other, and finally to the guests. The wedding was over. What had seemed like hours had been, as the Reverend had promised it would be, only a few minutes. The food had not even begun to cool.

We put all of Hetta's seals, as well as our own and those of the other witnesses, on the Chinese marriage certificate. We ate all the food and drank all the drink. The Reverend Mr. Feng got his nine dollars Mex., and Mr. Kepler had, by his own testimony, "a most interesting evening." But because, marriage or not, Aimee's father was still dying, and the soldiers, who were not to know there had been a wedding, were still in the house, I went home with the Empsons and played three-handed bridge until morning. And then I went to the consulate and paid my dollar, and subsequently locked among my most valuable documents a piece of stiff white paper with "U.S. Consular Service Marriage Certificate" printed in bold black type across the top. Typewritten underneath, making Aimee and me lawfully married in the eyes of the government of the United States, are the words "Rev. Joseph Feng of the Assemblies of God officiating."

WHITE FUNERAL, WHITE SOCKS

THE PRESENCE of the soldiers in the front courts would have been trouble enough for the family, but they also had the task of keeping old Mr. Yu, who was confined to the rooms of his private courtyard, from knowing of it. The family felt that if he should learn of such an invasion of the privacy of his home, his last days would be days of defeat instead of days spent in the peaceful contemplation of a respected career. Four days after our wedding, Mr. Yu died without ever knowing that his beloved garden had been desecrated and that his mansion and fortune were collapsing.

Between the fall of Peking and Mr. Yu's death, the family maintained his courtyard and rooms as they had always been, but everywhere else in the house they did their best to conceal any evidence of their remaining wealth. Windows that had cracked during the bombardment of the city were left unrepaired. Carpets were removed and hidden, along with paintings, porcelains, silk cushions, and tapestries. The members of the family all did what they could to increase the air of destitution. Cooking stoves were moved into the larger halls, and ashes were scattered on the floors. One of my wife's sisters found, in a storeroom, a rusty ice-cream freezer, which looked mechanical and proletarian, and put it in the middle of the main hall. And, as a final touch, Ninth Sister, the youngest, came home one day with a sock-knitting machine.

The machine was a boxed mechanism entirely mysterious to me. It was operated by a crank, and protruding from the top of the box were long needles, set in a circle. A skein of yarn was put into the machine, and when it was cranked, a knitted cylinder came off the needles. As far as I could make out, you just stopped cranking eventually, sewed up one end of the cylinder, and somehow got a serviceable sock, but I'm sure there must have been more to the operation than that. Anyway, the family agreed that the machine looked fine beside the ice-cream freezer, and, furthermore, they all felt that it allowed them to tell the Communists that they expected to earn a living by making socks.

I don't think all this camouflage fooled anyone. Although the family did succeed in making the place almost unlivable, they would have had to burn it to the ground to keep even the most obtuse police inspector from knowing that the beams and pillars were of the finest cedar, and that the tiles of the floors rivaled in blackness and smoothness those of the Imperial Palace. And I am sure they would even then have had to commit suicide en bloc to hide the fact that they were people trained in the art of spending money.

Actually, they might have saved themselves a good deal of trouble, because they reversed the process and restored the house when the old man died. They decided to give him a funeral in orthodox grand style, and this decision led them to feel that they wanted, after all, to hold on to their standard of living as long as they could. They had already restored the Hall of Ancient Pines at the time Aimee, the Fourth Miss Yu, and I were married—an event that automatically gave me the designation of Fourth Brother—and most of the rest of the job was done for the funeral. We had decided that it was best I not move into the mansion until the end of the forty-day mourning period.

I was with friends on the night of old Mr. Yu's death. Aimee telephoned me. When I arrived at the mansion gate, the

Communist soldiers were milling uncertainly about the front courtyard, aware that something had happened inside the house. A servant told me Aimee was at the well in the garden, and I set out, by way of a small door in the courtyard wall, to look for her. It was a moonless night and the garden was very black. A wind was shaking the high trees and rustling through the bamboo. Thinking of the old man newly dead, I might have been uneasy had it not been for the very ordinary horses of the soldiers stamping at their tethers in the darkness all around me.

A white stone path that began at the door ran past the well, and I had followed it for a considerable distance when I was startled to see someone in white coming toward me, carrying what looked like a raised umbrella. Then I heard the figure call, in Aimee's voice, "David, is that you?"

As she came closer, I could see that she really was carrying an umbrella, and a pail of water besides. Her white dress, I knew, was mourning attire. "The dead must be washed with water drawn at night," she said when I asked what she was doing. "The water must not be touched by the light of the sky, even the night sky. It is a custom."

We walked back to the door of the main courtyard together, past the bamboo and the trees and the horses. I wanted to say something comforting, but Aimee looked capable and in control of herself, and I could think of nothing that seemed right. When we had gone through the door, I heard weeping and chanting. Aimee stopped, and then suddenly began crying, "Ai ya! Ai yo!" and went toward the main hall. I followed, feeling bewildered and wondering if, as Fourth Brother, I should cry out, too.

The whole family and about twenty Buddhist monks were gathered in the hall. Aimee folded her umbrella and surrendered her bucket to one of her aunts, who carried it away. The relatives, including a number of people I had never seen before, were dressed in unhemmed gowns of unbleached muslin and were moaning and wailing. The monks were chanting the Feast of the Dead, and were making a good deal of noise with gongs, wooden blocks, and bells. Aimee brought me a white sash and tied it around my waist under my suit coat, and told me to sit down. The only people making no outcry or other noise were the servants. I saw one of them going out of the hall with the rusty ice-cream freezer in his arms. The sock-knitting machine was already gone. Other servants were cleaning, laying carpets, or polishing furniture. The wall mirrors, of which there were many, had been covered with sheets of white paper.

Actually, the old man's death had come as no shock to the family. It had been expected, and they knew that Mr. Yu would never have been able to approve of "New China," and that in a short time the inviolability of his own courtyard would have been shattered. They felt he was better out of it—honored in death rather than humiliated in life. And partly because, in their relief, they also felt guilty, and partly because they were uncertain of their own future, they had decided that the old man's funeral was to be a sort of symbol of the past as he had known it—a last flaring of gold-and-red pomp before they should all be submerged in the drab puritanism of the revolution.

After I had sat with the mourners for some time, Aimee took me outside into the cool night air. She explained that what I had been witnessing was the first-night wake, and that it would go on until morning. As a member of the family, I had honored her father by being present, but as a foreigner, I was not expected to stay the whole time. She told me that the ceremonies of the funeral would last for forty days, but that the most elaborate rites would take place on the third day. Then she walked with me through the still, empty courtyard. The family was waiting, she said, for the coffin, which was being brought from the ancestral family temple in the North City. Her father had bought it, as was

19

the custom, many years before, and the wood, a species of camphor, was of a quality and thickness now unobtainable. Every month for at least twenty years, a fresh layer of lacquer had been put on it.

We walked on, and just as we reached the main gate, the immense coffin arrived on the shoulders of six bearers, its surface black and sparkling in the light from their lanterns. One end of it was high, made to look like the stern of a Chinese junk, and its sides had been shaped like those of a boat, to enable it to cleave the black waters where the dead travel. As it came sliding darkly through the gate, the Communist soldiers, most of whom had been recruited from superstitious peasant stock, drew back, muttering, their eyes wide. Aimee touched the coffin as it passed, and a moment later we said good night. I walked away, and, outside the huge gate, turned back and saw her standing there, looking ghost-like in her white robe, watching me. The soldiers were in clumps about her, though they did not stand too close, and I could still see, behind her, the dark shape of the coffin receding into the darkness.

In the three days before the climax of the funeral rites, the Yu mansion changed considerably. Over all the tiled outdoor courts, box-shaped roofs of reed matting, looking something like large sheds, were erected on bamboo scaffolding. Framed panes of brightly painted glass were set in the sides of these, above the level of the surrounding buildings and galleries. In this way almost an acre of open courts was changed into lofty rooms smelling of straw and filled with golden-yellow dust.

I was in the house early on the second morning, when a Communist cadre came. In Western usage, the term applies to a number of men forming the skeleton of a larger group, but it is the approved Chinese Communist designation for one man acting as a sort of political commissar. This man arrived just as the workmen were beginning the day's construction and cleaning. He strode angrily about the courts watching the bustle, and after he had asked the workmen (most of them professional funeral caterers and descendants of funeral caterers, who took pride in their work and charged enormous prices) what they were doing and how much they were getting paid, he joined the soldiers and conferred with them. Presently, they produced from somewhere a flaking blackboard, and for the next hour the main courtyard rang with Communist hymns. The cadre wrote the first lines on the blackboard, and the soldiers shouted them and went on from there.

"Out of the East comes the sun, out of the East comes Mao Tse-tung," they sang. "In Red Leaf Village, the landlords are gone. Ai ya! The farmers dance and sing. Red Warriors liberate the south. The people are throwing flowers at their feet."

When the soldiers were done singing, they took out the paper-bound Communist catechisms that they all carried and, in response to the questions of the cadre, read aloud in their flat country accents.

"What is the place of the soldier in New China?"

"The soldier protects the people and drives the running dogs of imperialism from our shores."

"What is the Soviet Union?"

"The Soviet Union is China's big brother and is helping us drive the imperialist reactionaries into the sea."

After quite a lot of this, the soldiers all sat down on the folding campstools they carried strapped to their backs, and the cadre began barking out a lecture on the evils of bureaucratic capitalism and amassed wealth. "All this is the old, evil China," he said. He waved his arms as if to sweep away the mansion and the workmen. The soldiers glared about them. "All these people employed for one dead old man is a reactionary crime against New China!" The soldiers stirred, and snarled at the workmen. "But wait!" the cadre cried.

"They are doomed! We need not even push them! They are already dying from their own inner decay." The soldiers smiled complacently. "Watch them and learn!" said the cadre.

The climactic third day was bedlam. Since the principal rooms of the Yu mansion were in a direct line, separated by courtyards, and their main doors had been removed and the courtyard gates opened, one could look down a huge vista filled with wild but purposeful disorder.

In some of the courtyards, the caterers had set up tables for refreshments. In others, great bouquets of paper flowers and life-size paper figures of horses and servants, for the equipage of Mr. Yu in the other world, were being prepared. These would later be burned, to send them on their way. Meanwhile, ingots of gold paper, also for his use, were kept blazing in an iron brazier. A drum at the main gate, so huge that the man beating it had to stand on a ladder, was struck at intervals to announce the arrival of guests—one beat for a man, two for a woman. In two courtyards, there were chanting monks and Buddhist-temple orchestras composed of gongs, drums, trumpets, racks of bells, and hand-held reed organs. The Communist soldiers, dressed in uniforms of Yenan yellow, sat doggedly in the midst of the turmoil, eating pickled radishes and cooking vegetables over a coal-ball fire. (Coal balls are made by mixing coal dust and mud. They make a good fire, but leave enormous clinkers.) And in and out of halls and courtyards, through clouds of incense, wandered the guests. There were the Chinese ones, the declining aristocracy of Peking—silk-gowned ancient men with those elegant beards that only the Chinese can grow; their slender, white-faced, pomaded sons; and their first wives, second wives, concubines, and mistresses, smelling faintly of sandalwood, face powder, and soap. There were also foreign guests, who, in sunglasses and slacks, and loaded down with cameras, tripods, and light meters, seemed to be everywhere at once, snapping pictures. Most of them were friends of mine, whom the family had been happy to invite for the express purpose of getting pictures of the occasion taken, and, as a matter of fact, the pictures were to have a kind of historical value. Though nobody realized it at the time, this was to be the last of the great funerals for which—along with dust, duck, and opera—Peking was famous. Thereafter, the new government simply reassessed the property of any family foolish enough to produce the money for a funeral of such dimensions.

I was wearing a dark-blue Chinese gown, with a white sash—a symbol of limited mourning. I had had difficulty finding the white socks that gave a more formal appearance to a Chinese gown, because most of mine had, along with my summer clothes, been locked away in camphor chests that at the moment were inaccessible. So I had on a pair mismatched both in weave and in the degree of whiteness.

Deciding to go to the garden to escape the noise and confusion for a moment, I saw Ninth Sister through a window of one of the small inner rooms, and went inside to speak to her. She saw my socks almost immediately, and tears came to her eyes. "Your socks don't match," she said.

"I know," I said.

She began to cry. "Papa's dead and we're all becoming poor—even you, an American!" she said. She was only eighteen, and she looked very tiny and lost in her square-cut muslin mourning sack.

"Don't cry," I said to her. "Your father was an old man, and . . ."

"Oh, I'm not crying for Papa," she said. "I'm glad he's dead. He can never see what's happened. Elder Brother says that next month, after we finish paying for the funeral, we must give up all the servants but two. He told me I must remember to turn off lights, and he's already asked a man to cut down the big trees in the front court and sell them for wood, and he says he's going to raise pigs in the garden. Oh, I'm *glad* Papa's dead! He loved this house and the garden and the trees. I love them, too, and I wish I were dead with Papa."

There wasn't much I could say. The Yu family *were* poor. Their stocks and deposits had become so much paper, and even if they tried to stay together and keep the house, they would have to live very differently from the way they had lived before the revolution. "Don't worry," I told Ninth Sister. "Do as your brother says, and everything will be all right."

Actually, I didn't believe that anything would ever again be all right for them—their way of life was ending unconditionally—but she looked up, brushing away her tears.

"Yes," she said. "We are still the Yu family, and if we stay together, everything will still be as it used to be. I will help. I promise I will. I have a plan, too."

"You have? What plan?" I asked.

"I don't want to tell you now," she said, "but I've been thinking about it for a long time."

I didn't see Ninth Sister again until late that afternoon, when I was taking my place in a procession consisting of the family, the guests, the monks, and the orchestras. At its head marched a group of monks blowing ten-foot-long horns carried for them by little boys, who marched before them. The horns were to dispel evil spirits. Each could sound only one note, but, blown several at a time or all together, they produced uncanny harmonies. After the horns came the orchestras, playing, and then more monks, now quite hoarse but still chanting. Next came the spirit tower of Mr. Yu, borne on bamboo poles—a small paper pagoda in which was enshrined a fading framed photograph, taken some thirty years before, of Mr. Yu wearing a European suit and high collar.

Behind the spirit tower came the immediate family, and then the other relatives, all carrying bundles of lighted incense sticks and wearing white paper flowers. Mr. Yu's eldest son, as chief of the mourners, wore white net blinkers over his eyes, symbolizing a grief so deep as to make him unable to see. Although actually he could see, and could walk quite well, ceremony demanded that he be supported on either side by attendants. Every ten feet, he knelt on a cushion placed before him by an attendant, knocked his head on the ground three times, and wailed. He would then be helped to his feet and taken forward another ten feet. Behind the family, at a pace respectfully—and necessarily—slow, came the several hundred guests. They, too, carried incense and wore paper flowers.

At intervals in the procession were the paper servants and paper horses, held up on poles by funeral caterers. There was also a paper sedan chair, and there was a paper pleasure boat about fifteen feet long, complete in every detail. Through its windows I could see, among other surprising furnishings, paper tables with paper teacups on them, and a miniature paper model of an old-fashioned, round-topped Zenith radio.

The purpose of our procession was to burn all these paper objects, with the exception of Mr. Yu's photograph (but including the spirit tower itself), outside the walls of a nearby Buddhist temple. We reached it eventually, and the burning began. The pagoda was set on fire first, and when it began to collapse the other objects were thrown onto the fire one by one. It was macabre to see the very human-looking servants first curl in the heat of the fire and then burst into flame. Their faces and hands were of papier-mâché, and burned more slowly than their clothes. I thought of Joan of Arc, of medieval witches, and of the ancient funeral sacrifices of real servants, of which this ceremony was a discomforting survival.

One of the foreigners, trying for a photograph, got too close to the fire and suffered the loss of both his eyebrows. He was nearly burned more seriously, and I couldn't help thinking how astounded old Mr. Yu would have been if a foreigner with a camera in his hands and an assortment of leather pouches hanging from his shoulders had appeared out of the smoke and flame to assist him in the other world. He would surely have been at a loss to know what imbecility had come over his children, who were responsible for providing for his wants in that distant place.

Although, following the fire ceremony, old Mr. Yu's soul was gone, and was now presumably well provided for, his body, sealed in its coffin, still lay in the main hall of the house. A temporary partition screened the coffin, and in front of this was a table—a sort of altar—on which stood the old framed photograph of Mr. Yu. The coffin was to remain there forty days, during which offerings of various sorts, mostly food, incense, and ingots of gold paper, would be made at the altar. Then it was to be taken, with elaborate ceremony, in a brocade-and-silk-covered palanquin, to the family tombs outside the city.

I saw Ninth Sister only once in this waiting period. The Communist soldiers had finally been assigned official military barracks and were moving out. They were as happy to go as the family was to see them go. Elder Brother, for the sake of appearances, bowed them out the main gate, and they went marching off, their packs and campstools on their backs, frying pans and tin cups clanking at their belts. I found Ninth Sister standing in the litter of the rooms they had vacated and looking thoughtfully about. "The family doesn't want these rooms," she said. "I thought I might use them."

"What for?" I asked.

"You wait and see," she said, and, looking very pleased with herself, skipped away.

I went on to Aimee's rooms. I was still living with friends, for, though I would have liked to accept the family's invitation to move, with Aimee, into a suite in the mansion, I couldn't bring myself to do so with Mr. Yu's body only a few courts away and the family still in mourning.

Aimee had prepared dinner for the two of us that day. She had made a dish of which she was justly proud—diced pork and fried peanuts, done in some secret way. I had eaten it before, and knew that it was undeniably special. Now she served it, and I took the first bite expectantly. "It's not quite the same today," I said hesitantly. "There doesn't seem to be as much flavor as usual."

Aimee smiled. "I know," she said. "Papa ate it first."

I choked. "Papa's dead," I said.

"I put the food on the altar in front of his spirit picture," Aimee said. "We give everything to Papa now before we eat it. But Papa eats only the flavor. We eat the rest. Nothing's tasted right for weeks."

I'm afraid I was being callous, but I was growing weary of not living with my wife, and of the suffocating clouds of incense and the smell of burning paper that constantly filled the house. A tremendous number of ingots of gold paper were still being burned for Mr. Yu, and I wondered what the old man could possibly be doing with all that gold, and whether it was absolutely necessary that he take the very flavor out of my mouth. "Please, Aimee," I said, "aren't the forty days up?"

Aimee said that the forty days were indeed up, but that the family was having trouble with the authorities, who refused to grant a permit to move Mr. Yu's body out of the city. They also refused to permit any sort of procession. Forty days before, the family would not have needed a permit. The new government was taking hold rapidly. The authorities had explained that Mr. Yu couldn't be buried without one of the new death certificates, but insisted that as he had already been dead for forty days, they couldn't issue one. It was no concern of theirs that at the time the old man died few residents of the city had ever heard of a death certificate.

And, finally, the officials had pointed out that if the family had not been observing old-fashioned, feudalistic customs, they would have buried Mr. Yu properly right after he died and there would have been no trouble for anyone.

After two more weeks of waiting and asking, the family was given a carefully worded death certificate, which said that the cause of death was unknown and which seemed to imply that, for all the authorities could say, the old man might have been done in by his sons and daughters. Two days later, the permit to move the body out of the city came through, along with a burial permit, but there was no permit to hold a procession. All the delay and harassment had been, I believe, simply the government's way of asserting its authority. So the end of the funeral ceremonies was at hand at last, and the great black coffin was loaded without much ceremony into the back of an open truck for its final journey.

Elder Brother rode with it. He was still dressed in muslin and had put his blinkers on again, and clutched in his hands were the documents without which the truck couldn't have been driven around the block.

A few other members of the family were to follow the truck in a rented Buick—the second son, two of Mr. Yu's sisters, the only one of his brothers then living in the city, the eldest daughter, and Aimee. Though this was intended to be only a small group of elders, Aimee was taken along because, as the most eloquent member of the family, she had been involved in the negotiations for the permits and might be needed to make explanations at the city gates. Suddenly, when everything seemed ready, there was a great flurry of excitement, incense was hastily burned, and old Aunt Yu, one of Mr. Yu's two sisters, was expelled from the Buick. As it drove away, she stood beside me looking after it and sniffling. "What did you do?" I asked her.

"I stepped over water," she said. "It rained last night, and there was a puddle. It's very unpropitious to step over water on the way to a burial."

"Why?" I asked.

She looked surprised. "I wonder," she said, and went into the house.

A short while later, I was sitting alone and rather sad in the Eastern Study, when I heard a tap at the door and Ninth Sister's voice asking, "Fourth Brother, are you there?"

"Come in!" I called.

She came, holding something behind her back and looking wise. "I have a present for you. It's my surprise," she said.

She thrust a pair of white socks at me. "I made them. These are my first. I learned to work the machine all by myself. We must buy more machines, and then the whole family can make them. We'll have a factory."

She was quite serious. I put on the socks, feeling old and somewhat abashed by my forebodings in the face of her resilience. I could leave China. I could take my wife and get out any time I wanted to, but Ninth Sister was already planning to build a life for herself, to see that her family made its way in a society she could not yet begin to understand. The socks were good ones, and were the right size, too.

"Thank you," I said. "You made them very well."

In the fashion of polite Chinese, she answered, "I cannot dare presume so."

ALL THE EMPEROR'S HORSES

My CHINESE father-in-law had been well known not only as a former Chief Justice of the Chinese Supreme Court but also as a collector of antiques. His name was a legend in Peking's famous Liu Li Ch'ang, a street where the finest art was bought and sold over cups of tea in back rooms filled with the smell of old woods and paper, and even people who cared little or nothing for antiques knew that he had once swapped a country estate in the Western Hills for a pair of porcelain wine cups.

When he died, he left to his children his Peking mansion, in which his family had lived for generations; an enormous, uncatalogued collection of antiques, including the porcelain wine cups; the family's ancestral temple, in the North City; and a trunkful of obsolete currency and worthless stock.

Perhaps the weakest part of the Yu mansion was the roofs, which were of tiles cemented with mud. Windblown seeds would take root in the mud, and grass, or even trees, would spring up, eventually dislodging the tiles and causing leaks in the roof. Weeding such a roof takes scaffolding, skilled workmen, and money, and therefore the family had for some time allowed the greenery over their heads to grow unhindered. Meanwhile, the enormous garden had also run wild. Its rock pools stood dry. The red and turquoise lacquer on pillars, balustrades, and gates peeled off. The elaborate painting under the mansion's eaves flaked and fell, and everywhere in the cool, dark rooms—many of them locked and unused, since most of the servants had been let go—porcelains and embroideries, paintings and parquetry gathered dust.

It was into the Eastern Study that Aimee and I moved. The suite consisted of a bedroom, a library, a study, and a reception room, and had in the past been old Mr. Yu's retreat for contemplation and afternoon naps. We had the responsibility of keeping the suite in order, and, in addition, Aimee had considerable trouble cooking for us. She could make a number of showy dishes, such as one might find on the menu of an expensive Peking restaurant, but she couldn't boil rice, and since the problems of cooking left her little time for general housework, we felt fortunate in being able to get the gatekeeper's twelve-year-old daughter, who was called Little Blackie, to help us with it at least once a week.

From the beginning, I felt at home in those rooms, filled with objects that kept alive the values of the old, traditional China. I felt that despite the revolution and the rumblings of war, I was living near the timeless heart of Cambaluc itself. Like boxes within boxes, and puzzles within puzzles, Peking's walled courtyards lie one within another, all surrounded ultimately by the sloping walls and fortress towers of the Outer City. And, sitting in a box in what seemed to me the center of it all—the old man's dusty and neglected study—I often felt unreasonably complacent, convinced that what I had there was more real than what lay outside, because it had not changed.

Shortly after Aimee and I moved into the Eastern Study, Elder Brother, now head of the family, decided to catalogue the antiques in the house, and we were given the task of listing those in our suite of rooms. This wasn't easy. We had to ferret everything out of drawers, cabinets, and chests, and then we had to decide which pieces were antique and which weren't. As far as I was concerned, almost everything in the rooms—including the hand-blown electric-light bulbs under tasseled silk shades—could safely have been listed.

There was no question about the paintings; they all went on the list, as did all the porcelain. But there was another, and to me far more interesting, list we could have made, of some valueless but delightful objects we turned up in the course of our search. It would have looked like this:

1. Three enameled silver fingernail guards.
2. One pair of gold-filigreed glass jars, filled with snuff, and wrapped in blue silk and packed in individual pearwood boxes.
3. One ivory shovel, six inches long, inlaid with coral and turquoise. Use unknown.
4. One *ku-ch'in* (a silk-stringed zither, sometimes called a horizontal harp) of black lacquer.
5. Four double-eyed and two triple-eyed peacock plumes, meant to be worn in the hats of mandarins.
6. Three rosebud-painted spittoons.

Eventually, we came to the bronze incense burners. They were the most important objects in the Eastern Study. There were seventeen of them, of which fourteen were displayed, and the old man had been famous among connoisseurs throughout China for being their owner. The largest, about the size and shape of an ordinary saucepan, sat in the middle of a long table that stood against one wall, and six smaller bronze vessels were ranged along the table, three on each side of it. Seven others were symmetrically set out on a square table set flush against the larger one.

The unique thing about these incense burners was that they had always to be kept burning. They had been in Aimee's charge from the time her father became bedridden, and he had given her detailed instruction in their history and care. Unlike the ancient, intricately patterned, and patina-encrusted Chinese bronze sacrificial vessels that are in the world's museums, these bronzes were clean and smooth and comparatively new, having been cast only five hundred years ago. However, according to Aimee, their like had never been made before or since.

One day, she told me their story. In the reign of the Hsüan Te Emperor, in the Ming dynasty, one of the palace buildings, in which were many gold images, burned to the ground. The building was a complete loss, its smoking ruins later yielding up only numerous lumps of melted gold. At about this time, the court received as tribute from Burma a shipment of fine red copper, and almost simultaneously some ground rubies arrived from Turkestan. These three events inspired a conscientious official to memorialize the throne.

"May it please Your Majesty," he said, in effect, "gold is no more or less valuable than its market price. Copper ore, unrefined, is no better than the common soil with which the empire abounds. Even ground rubies, although of some medicinal value, can be put to use only occasionally. However, mixed together by the alchemist's art, and combined with various other substances that are also plentiful and at hand, bronze objects of unexcelled beauty can be created. As there is no greater evidence of virtue than the proper observance of rites and ceremonies, and as the palace is at the moment in great need of incense burners, I take my life in my hands and tremblingly suggest that Your Majesty order the most skilled artisans to produce incense burners with these ingredients."

Hsüan Te Emperor was delighted, and the project was carried out. The incense burners appeared one by one, each more beautiful than the last, from the bronze works, as they were cast, and none of them was allowed to cool completely.

At this point, Aimee interrupted herself to explain to me how the Chinese burn incense. The incense itself is never set afire. The bowl of an incense burner is first filled with a fine, powdery gray-white ash, preferably the ash of incense. Then a tiny brick of charcoal is buried under the ash, where, with its oxygen supply cut to the minimum, it continues to smolder for as long as three or four days. After the coal is buried, the incense—a chip of sandalwood or aloewood, for example—is placed in the bowl, on the surface of the ash, where it grows slowly hotter and hotter, until it begins to smoke, darken, and curl. Incense burned in this way lasts the longest and gives the richest aroma.

These incense burners, then, had been kept constantly hot. The burning charcoal core in them had been replaced every two or three days. Some of the Hsüan Te burners had gone out, before they came into Aimee's father's hands, but these fourteen had never cooled in five hundred years.

They were magical objects, glowing and shimmering like jewels, no two alike. Some were red; others were speckled with iridescent green or with twinkling bits of ruby or gold. One had a smooth gold surface, incredibly bright and shining. When Aimee had explained their origin to me, she went to a cabinet and brought out an incense burner of exquisite shape but of a dull, brassy color. "This is what would happen if the fire went out," she said.

"Couldn't you build another fire in it?" I asked.

"Of course," Aimee said, "but nothing would happen. Once the burner is allowed to grow entirely cold, the color fades and no later heat can bring it back."

The cold, empty-bellied little incense pot seemed tragic to me. Because I knew what it must have been like when it was alive, I could see that it was dead, and I was able to understand for the first time that the rooms in which I lived, the tiny ivory shovel, the porcelain wine cups, and the silk-stringed harp were dead as well. Never having seen them alive, I had failed to see that this was so.

Days passed, in the Eastern Study. We made our lists. Aimee fired her pots. Sometimes I plucked at the silk-stringed harp and listened to its seven melancholy notes. Sometimes I sat gazing in awe at the wall, lined with blue clothbound books. Without opening them, I knew their pages, covered with vertical lines of black characters speaking eternally of blue-green winds and of the ancient man of virtue. Gradually I found myself being attracted more and more strongly by the mystery of the little ivory shovel. We had come across it in a drawer of old letters and papers, which gave no clue to its use. Aimee had shown it to the members of the family, asking if anyone knew what it was for. No one did. Even old Aunt Chin, who was supposed to know everything, had come up with no better idea than that it must have been used to shovel up some precious substance, like powdered incense, or snuff, or gold dust. But I wanted to bring something alive again in those rooms that, except for the burning pots, seemed so dead to me. Nobody could play the harp, nobody took snuff any more, and smelling incense was out of fashion. Whether or not I would ever be able to use the shovel didn't matter; I merely wanted to know what it was for. I took to carrying it with me in my breast pocket, beside my fountain pen, as I might, suddenly and without thinking, find myself taking it out and using it as it was meant to be used.

One afternoon, I came home and found the mansion's main gate closed. "Lao Ma!" I called to the gatekeeper. "I'm back!" There was no response. "Little Blackie!" I called, hoping his daughter was there. "Open the gate!" Still no one came.

I knew that the gate was supposed never to be left untended. I went to the gatehouse and, standing on tiptoe, discovered that I could just bring my eyes level with the high, paper-covered, latticed window that opened on the street. It took me a while to find a place where the paper was torn, but I did, and then I saw with one eye Little Blackie standing near the door. She was listening, and smiling to herself, and didn't realize I was looking at her. "Little Blackie!" I yelled as loud as I could. "Why don't you open the gate?"

She gave a start, ran out the door, and disappeared into

the inside courts of the house. She had never behaved like that before.

Beginning to be angry, I picked up a handful of small stones and, standing out in the road, pitched them over the gate. I heard them clatter down the gate's steep roof and fall into the tiled courtyard. Then someone came running, the gate bars were lifted, and Lao Ma, panting and apologetic, swung the gate open. I started to ask him what had come over his child, and then thought better of it. They were the family's servants, not mine, and it was better to let the family deal with them. I decided, however, that I would tell Aimee what had happened. I asked where she was, and Lao Ma said she was in the garden.

I found her sitting in a lawn chair beside one of the rock-bordered pools. She would have presented a very poetic picture, leaning forward and gazing raptly into the pool, had I not known that it was dry and that several pigs lived at the bottom of it. The pigs were Elder Brother's most recent enterprise. Even before I got to the dry pool, I could hear that it was their mealtime. Aimee looked up. "Listen," she said. "Isn't it an interesting sound? More like an elephant than a pig." Aimee had never heard or seen an elephant, as far as I was aware.

"Elephants eat very quietly," I said, not knowing whether they did or not.

We walked away, and I told her about Little Blackie's peculiar behavior.

"She's been very impolite lately," Aimee said. "She's begun to go to school."

"Wouldn't school have the opposite effect?" I asked.

"They don't learn the same things in school now that they used to," Aimee said. "Her teachers know she's the daughter of one of our servants, and they've been teaching her not to obey us or believe anything we say. They tell her we are outmoded. One time, she even asked me if I was Chinese, and when I told her I was, she got angry. She didn't believe me. She asked why I had married a foreigner, if I was Chinese, and why I didn't work, and why I wore a fur coat made from the skins of thousands of dead animals. I tried to talk sense to her, but it's impossible. She just repeats what she is taught at school. Well, I'll speak to her father. It's his duty to scold her, if he's not afraid of her."

Aimee and I left the house together about four the next afternoon. Little Blackie, whose father, I knew, had both scolded and slapped her because of the gate incident, was sitting on a marble stepping block just inside the gate. I thought she might run away when she saw us coming, but she sat still, staring at us—trying her best, I couldn't help feeling, to kill us by the power of the evil eye.

We had tea with friends and dinner in a restaurant in the South City, and returned home late. Lao Ma, awakened from his sleep, let us in. We did not see his daughter. The huge mansion, with so many of its rooms empty, seemed very dark. We made our way by flashlight along dark verandas, through archways and doors and echoing courtyards, to our own rooms, in the Eastern Study. Aimee switched on the lights. "I feel uncomfortable," she said. "Something bad is going to happen."

She was wrong. It had already happened, though we didn't know it until the next morning.

Aimee always got up early. That morning, I heard her cry out from the sitting room, "Ai ya! Ai ya!" I rushed there and found her looking with horror at one of the smaller incense burners, which she was holding in her hand. She quickly put it down and picked up another. Then she touched all the rest of them. "They're all cold!" she wailed, and collapsed in a chair.

They looked cold. All the color and life was gone, leaving

them the color of a brass doorknob. I picked one burner up. The ash in the center was slightly damp; water had been poured into it. We found that each pot had been watered just enough to put out its fire.

Aimee was completely demoralized, and I was staggered myself, not only at the thought of the beauty that had been destroyed but at the idea of five centuries of tending and firing wiped out in the space of seconds. The incense burners were no longer an anachronism in these rooms. The last illusion of a link with the past had been broken, and all the emperor's horses and all the emperor's men couldn't put the old China together again.

I sat down beside Aimee. "Who did it?" I asked.

"That girl, of course," she answered. "I'm going to kill her. I don't care what happens to me. I'll kill her!" But she didn't move, or even raise her head, as she spoke.

The pots were left sitting in their places on the table for the rest of the time Aimee and I lived in that house, but Aimee never touched them again. As far as I know, Little Blackie was not punished—not by Aimee, at least, and not by the family. But Lao Ma was a man of character and strong principles, and it would have been impossible for him to remain in the house. He and his daughter packed up and left within a week.

Long afterward, one of Aimee's sisters found an ivory birdcage packed away in a chest in one of the storehouses. It was decorated with turquoise and coral in exactly the same style as my little shovel, which, I understood at last, had been used to clean out bird droppings from the bottom of the cage. But there was no excitement in the discovery. It didn't seem to matter any more.

CRIMINALS, CADRES, AND COOKS

THE COMMUNIST army called itself the Liberation Army, and after the surrender the foreigners remaining in Peking fell, merely for convenience, into the habit of speaking of events as having occurred "pre-liberation" or "post-liberation." My own experience was sharply divided between the two. Pre-liberation, I taught English at the National Tsinghwa University, six miles from Peking, and had a house on the campus; post-liberation, I wasn't allowed to teach English anywhere, and lived in the home of Aimee's family, in Peking. The story of Lao Pei, my cook, is also separated into two parts by the "liberation."

Most foreigners in Peking had some sort of servant trouble sooner or later. Pre-liberation, the stories of these troubles were standard conversation at any gathering. The servant was invariably a cook. He could cook French, Russian, Chinese, or Mongolian food to perfection, but he had idiosyncrasies. He slept with carving knives under his pillow, or he had fainting spells, or he saw ghosts. Eventually, he went berserk, wielding a knife or a meat chopper. On being dismissed, he told his secret: he was a victim of the 1911 revolution. He had been a Manchu bannerman—a retainer of the imperial family, or a noble subsidized by them—or even a prince of the old nobility, and was now reduced to common labor.

Although Lao Pei's father *had* been a bannerman, Lao Pei himself was a generation removed from the tragedies of the 1911 revolution, and I felt that he was a cut above the typical foreigner's cook. He knew some English, and was a superb cook, too, being a master of anything from *shashlik* to that work of patient love, Peking Dust—roasted chestnuts ground to a powder, poured into a mold of glazed berries, and topped with spun sugar and whipped cream. But soon after he came to me he began to do unpleasant things. I found that he had been killing chickens by driving a long needle slowly through their brains. He sometimes banged his head against the rockery in my garden until blood dripped from his hair. He was overwhelmed, he explained, by the woes of China. He moved a very young wife into his room behind my kitchen, and often beat her. I could hear her screams all over the house, but when I went to the kitchen, I would hear her laughing softly with Lao Pei in their room. One midnight, he came to my bedroom, woke me out of a deep sleep, and asked, "Did you call, sir?"

These incidents might have disturbed me less if my friends had not warned me of the knife- or chopper-wielding stage sure to follow. I finally decided to let Lao Pei go. I paid him most of a month's salary, and told him I wouldn't need him any longer. I had no real grounds, but he didn't seem to mind. He took his money and left. This was in 1948.

One evening early in the summer of 1949, I first saw the post-liberation Lao Pei. With Aimee, I was window-shopping along a street that, having wide, tree-lined sidewalks and Westernized shops, was a favorite promenade of foreigners and Chinese alike. The new regime had changed it only a little. The many signs printed in English were still there. One of them read, HOLLYWOOD BEAUTY SALON, SPECIALISTS IN HAIR CURVATION AND SCIENTIFIC HAIR DISCOLORATION. The Shanghai Department Store had become a government-operated New China Bookstore, however, and the Sea Dragon Shoe and Gold Shop would no longer exchange American dollars into yuan. Occasionally, as Aimee and I strolled, we passed a pair of newly arrived Russians. The

Russians were easy to spot, first because they were always in pairs, and then because without exception they wore wide trousers, which flapped about their ankles.

We were passing the sentry boxes flanking the entrance to the Military Police Headquarters when a beggar stepped in front of me and pushed a smeared card into my hand. These cards, lettered in Chinese on one side and English on the other, were common. They described the beggar's misfortunes, and I found them more compelling than most other gambits, but, having been trapped into reading them too often, I tried to give this one back unread. Then I recognized the beggar. He was Lao Pei, thin and incredibly dirty. We looked at each other a moment before he said "Mr. Tu!" (my Chinese name), and I said "Lao Pei!" and my wife drew a startled breath, wondering what kind of Chinese friends I had made before she knew me.

"I thought you had left China," Lao Pei said.

I read his card. It began, "One year I give American Imperialist making cook." After naming me as the American, it went on to say that I had refused to pay his salary and that, because I was a white man, and because the white man had controlled China at that time, he had been forced to work on for me in fear and misery, and for nothing. It declared that I had fled China before the justice of the advancing People's Armies could catch up with me, and had left poor Lao Pei exploited and unpaid, to seek what justice he might on the streets of Peking.

There was more, but I had read enough. I passed the card, Chinese side up, to my wife. I knew what I was up against. For the past month, the Peking *People's Daily* had been reporting that foreigners throughout China were being sued by their servants for back pay or other compensation. According to the paper, these foreigners had invariably starved their servants, worked them from sunup to midnight, beaten them when they became sick, cursed them when they asked for

41

their pay, and threatened them with prison when they tried to leave their jobs. No servant had been able to obtain justice from the police and courts of the old regime—the "running-dog" hirelings of the foreigners—but now, under the Communists, justice was for the people. In every case, the *Daily* reported, the servant had won his suit and the foreigner had either paid or gone to prison. The only thing that had so far prevented Lao Pei from taking me to court was the fact that he thought I had left China.

Holding tight to my arm, he put his face close to mine. "Will you pay me?" he asked.

Aimee looked at me, bewildered. "Surely you paid him?" she asked, in English.

"Of course I paid him," I answered, in Chinese. "This is all a lie. He's trying to"—there was a particular word I wanted, but I couldn't think of it—"to blackmail me," I said.

"Trying to blackmail you, am I?" Lao Pei yelled. "Here are the police, right here!" He pulled me toward the entrance to the Military Police Headquarters. "Come in and see if I'm blackmailing you!"

The way he said "Come in and see" sounded to me as if he had the disposition of his case all arranged. I turned to look for Aimee, but she was already inside the headquarters gate and halfway up the steps of the building, loudly demanding to know who was in charge. She had had a good deal of experience with the Communist authorities, having been involved in disputes over the soldiers they had quartered in her family's house, over property taxes, and over police permits of one kind or another, and she had told me that they always showed her respect if she talked louder than they did.

Someone ran out of the building and said, "This way, Miss," and led Aimee inside. I followed with Lao Pei still holding on to my arm.

———

Inside headquarters, the three of us were taken down a hall to a square, windowless room lined with benches. Four or five policemen, their rifles propped carelessly beside them, were lounging on one of the benches, smoking and talking. They fell silent when they saw us, and stared at us suspiciously; I noticed that they seemed just as suspicious of Lao Pei as they were of Aimee and me. "Don't speak Chinese," Aimee warned me, in English. "You might say something wrong. If they think you can't speak Chinese, I can do your talking for you."

"I heard you," Lao Pei said, in his own language. "His Chinese is as good as mine. Let him talk for himself."

A small, sturdily built officer came into the room, and immediately all the policemen rose to their feet. Lao Pei, after much bowing and scraping, whispered his accusations into the man's ear. Everyone waited. "He's an American," Lao Pei finished accusingly, but no one made any move to put manacles on my wrists or take special steps to restrain me.

"I will speak for my husband," Aimee said. "His Chinese is very poor."

"That's not true!" Lao Pei shouted. "He speaks Chinese like a Chinese!"

"Mind your own business," Aimee answered. "I'm his wife and I ought to know."

"I don't even know you," Lao Pei said to Aimee. "Why don't you stay out of this?"

"You're trying to extort him," Aimee said. "Extort"— "*nguh*"—was the word I had wanted earlier. It is used as a transitive verb, with the victim as object.

Aimee and Lao Pei went on arguing, and after a few moments the officer interrupted to say that the Military Police had no jurisdiction in a civil dispute. The proper courts were closed, he told us, and we would have to wait until morning.

"But he'll get away! I'll never find him again!" Lao Pei protested. "At least keep him here for the night!"

The officer repeated that he had no jurisdiction over our case and no grounds for holding me, and the three of us were led back outside. Lao Pei was beside himself. I wanted nothing more than to get into a pedicab and go home, but he had hold of my coat. Aimee called a pedicab man. "Don't take him anywhere!" Lao Pei shouted to him. "He's a criminal trying to run away!"

Aimee turned on Lao Pei. "Oh, you dead devil!" she said, using the strongest curse she ever allowed herself in Chinese. Lao Pei dropped my coat. "Come to the West Four, Number Three, Crooked Hair Family Lane, tomorrow morning, and we'll go to court together," she said, getting into the pedicab. "We're not afraid of you."

I got quickly into a cab that had come up behind hers, and we were rolled away before Lao Pei could think what to do.

That night, Aimee and I held a council of war. I said that if Lao Pei really needed money it might be best just to give him something and get rid of him. Aimee said no. If I did that, I would lose face by yielding to him, particularly after I had been insulted on the street. Yielding would also imply that I was guilty. Besides, if I paid him out of court, I would have no guarantee that he wouldn't try to do the same thing again. And finally, we needed the money almost as much as he did. I had lost my job at the university and, as I had no sympathy for the new Communist government, it seemed unlikely that I could get another, and Aimee's family's fortune had dwindled away since the Communists came to power. On the other hand, there was nothing at all to prevent Lao Pei from getting work; for one thing, he could cook Russian style, and all the arriving Russians were hiring cooks.

We decided to contest Lao Pei's claim. We hoped that Aimee's father's name would still have influence in a court of law. Most of Peking's pre-liberation white-collar government employees, including judges, were still in their old jobs and, except for having to attend daily meetings for indoctrination and self-criticism, were not interfered with very much by the Communists. Many of the older judges had been friends of my father-in-law, and the younger ones at least knew and respected his name. Still, there was no getting around the fact that he had held office under the old regime. We might be given a sympathetic hearing as the daughter and son-in-law of a respected friend, or we might be treated merely as representatives of a bureaucratic-capitalist family. We would have to take our chances. Aimee telephoned the Central Ministry of Justice to ask where we should go to settle the matter of Lao Pei's demand, and the ministry referred her to a local court not far from where we lived.

Next morning, our gateman reported that Lao Pei was already waiting outside the main gate of the house, and a few minutes later the three of us—Aimee, Lao Pei, and I—bounced off down the street in three pedicabs and presently pulled up at the local court. The gate of the court looked like the street gate of any private house in Peking except for a plaque hanging beside it, which identified it as a Municipal Court of Law. We all got out of our pedicabs and entered. After some difficulty, we found the right courtroom.

The room was divided in two by a wooden railing and, where that ended, a shoulder-high counter behind which sat the judge. We were the only litigants there. Across the railing from us were a number of court clerks, sitting at desks. The judge and the clerks were all dressed in blue cotton uniforms, called *Kan-pu i-fu*—cadre suits—because they were originally worn by those political commissars. These suits were rapidly becoming the national dress of China. The clerks were half-heartedly sipping tea and sorting great piles of paper stacked on their desks.

Lao Pei stepped up to the judge and spoke, bringing his charges against me, but he did less bowing than he had done when he addressed the police officer the day before. He addressed the judge several times as "Comrade," and referred to "our people's China" and "the foreign imperialists."

The judge sat listening and saying quietly, "Hmm, hmm, hmm," and when Lao Pei had finished, he asked, "Why didn't you file suit a year ago, when all this happened?"

"But our Liberation Army hadn't come yet," Lao Pei said. "The courts and officials were all on the side of the foreigners."

"I didn't think we were too bad," said the judge, looking around.

"Oh, not you, Comrade!" Lao Pei cried. "I mean the corrupt officials we had before liberation."

"I was an official before liberation," the judge said. "In fact, I was a judge, right here."

"Oh!" said Lao Pei.

"Why didn't you quit when you weren't paid?" the judge went on.

Lao Pei looked uncomfortable. "I was afraid to quit," he said.

"Why?"

"Because he is an American."

"What could an American do to you?" asked the judge.

"He could have put me in jail."

The judge looked at me. "Are you the person he's talking about?" he asked.

I started to answer, but Aimee cut in. "Yes, he is," she said.

"Who are *you*?" the judge asked her.

"I'm his wife," Aimee said.

"Why doesn't he speak for himself?"

"His Chinese is very bad," she said.

"That's not true," said Lao Pei.

"Shut up!" said the judge. "You've had your say." He turned back to Aimee. "Where are you from?" he asked her.

"I'm the fourth daughter of the Yu family of Crooked Hair Family Lane," she answered.

"Are you one of Justice Yu's daughters?" the judge asked.

Every head in the court turned in Aimee's direction. "Yes," she said.

"I heard one of his daughters had married an American," the judge said. "So this is your husband? That's interesting. Well, let's find out what the trouble is."

So Aimee told him the whole story—how long I had employed Lao Pei, what I had paid him per month, and when I had fired him and why. She wound up by describing how he had tried to "extort" me the day before.

"This must all be put down on paper," the judge said. He had a number of blank forms before him, and now he began filling some of them out. He remarked that before liberation he could pass judgment himself, but that now the record of every case had to be submitted for a verdict to the Central Ministry of Justice. The old legal code had been abolished and the new one was still being written. In the meantime, the courts had been stripped of almost all their authority. He pointed out that our case depended on one man's word against another's, and that there was almost no way to determine who was telling the truth except by comparing the plausibility of the two stories. He didn't mind telling us, he said, that he would make a recommendation in my favor, although he couldn't guarantee what the ministry's decision would be. At any rate, there would be no verdict for two weeks or so. The ministry was very busy.

For the next hour, Aimee and I helped the judge fill out forms. When they were completed, he told us that after a decision had been reached, we would be summoned by mail to reappear in court. We thanked him and left. Lao Pei went his way alone.

During the next few weeks, friends occasionally told me that they had seen Lao Pei begging on the street, but then the city government put on a strong campaign to stop begging, and he disappeared. Aimee and I waited a month without word from the court, and I began to wonder if the judge's recommendation in my favor, and possibly the fact that I was the son-in-law of a former justice, had blocked action. I was beginning to consider the whole affair closed when I met Lao Pei once more.

Again it was evening, and Aimee and I were shopping in the large open market on the Glacis—the old polo grounds—just outside the battered walls of the former legation quarter. Almost anything could be bought there, from jewelry, curios, old clothes, and used phonograph records to slowly deteriorating United States Army supplies that had got into the Chinese black market four or five years earlier. We had just bought a can of powdered milk and were haggling over the price of a coral-and-turquoise Mongolian ring when someone yanked at my arm. I turned and saw Lao Pei accompanied by two brawny, dark-faced soldiers. They were hung all over with tin cups, guns, grenades, and pouches, and in the failing light they looked incredibly cruel and stupid. I wondered if they might not be two of his friends, masquerading as soldiers, who were planning to take me off somewhere and either beat me up or kill me. When they indicated that they wanted to take me over toward the wall of the old legation quarter, where there were fewer people, I became alarmed.

"Don't take her," Lao Pei said, pointing to Aimee.

"You cannot not take me," Aimee said. "Where he goes, I go."

Lao Pei shrugged, and the men led us into the twilight shadows under the wall.

The five of us came eventually to a large shed built of woven mats, and went inside. The warm interior was partitioned into sections and was bright with electric lights. I saw about ten people there, a few of them dressed in blue cadre suits.

At that time, the new People's Courts were just being set up throughout Peking at points where business and traffic were heavy. This was one of them. Unlike the regular courts, they were empowered to deliver verdicts, and Lao Pei, impatient at the ministry's delay, had brought his case here. The People's Courts delivered a kind of quick, rough justice that helped fill the gap while the regular legal machinery was being overhauled. They were staffed by magistrates trained under Communist Party surveillance, and they made the law available to people too uneducated or too timid to bring a complaint before a proper court.

We were able to get some idea of how the system worked by watching the case that preceded ours. It involved the proprietor of a secondhand-bicycle stall, an elderly customer of his, and a young man who stood holding a bicycle with a broken steering bar. The young man had left his bicycle at the stall to be sold on a commission basis. It had been sold, but the customer had brought it back an hour later with its steering bar broken and had demanded a refund. The stallkeeper had refused to give him one, saying that the original owner was responsible for the weakened condition of the steering bar.

The case was heard by three examiners, who then deliberated and passed judgment. The bicycle was returned to the young man, and the proprietor was made to give the customer back his money. The customer was asked to pay 5 percent of his refund to the young man as damages. The young man was then asked to pay 25 percent of his damages to the stallkeeper to compensate him for his trouble. It was far from being an orthodox legal decision, but all three parties to the quarrel went away apparently satisfied.

Lao Pei, Aimee, and I were then presented to the court. Aimee and I were placed on one side of a mat partition and Lao Pei on the other, and for the third time all our formal charges and countercharges were heard. When these were finished, the examiners asked questions, stepping back and forth from one side of the mat to the other, repeating a question here and asking for further details there, in an attempt to find some discrepancy in the testimony.

They were polite and friendly until Aimee became so insistent about my inability to speak Chinese that she would not allow me to say how old I was. They felt that if I had been living in China since 1946, teaching in a Chinese university, and still could not give my age in Chinese, I must be badly retarded. I decided it was time to confess. "As a matter of fact, I speak well enough," I said, in Chinese. "It's only that I don't understand legal terms and might make a serious mistake in answering important questions."

All the examiners beamed at me as if I were a baby who had just spoken its first word. "Such an intelligent husband," one of them said to Aimee, and they all beamed at her, too.

From then on, the court was ours. Lao Pei didn't have a chance. "He's not a good man," one examiner told me confidentially. "He lies."

On the other hand, he said, Lao Pei really didn't have any money, and just for old times' sake I ought to give him something. They all agreed that if I did, they would make him sign a legal waiver of all claims, and I would never have any trouble again.

I asked how much they would suggest that I pay. They considered among themselves for a few moments, and decided that 20 percent of what he was asking would be about right. Luckily, I had enough money with me to pay the sum then and there. Lao Pei, after some hesitation, signed the waiver, and the court gave it to me.

I saw Lao Pei just once more, about two months later. I was riding in a pedicab on the Avenue of Long Peace, which at that time was being widened in preparation for the constant parades that were to follow the inauguration of the People's Republic. Gangs of prisoners were at work on the road, carrying stones and pouring tar. They were all dressed in blue cadre uniforms with large numbers painted in whitewash on the backs. Fine clouds of Peking's pervasive dust hung about them.

I was watching the prisoners' faces as my pedicab passed, and suddenly I saw Lao Pei. He was in a marching line, and he looked fatter than when I had last seen him. Like the rest, he was singing one of the new Communist songs without much enthusiasm. So the jails had got him at last! He had been picked up for begging, I suppose, or perhaps for another extortion, this time with a less vulnerable victim. My pedicab passed too quickly for him to notice me. As I crossed the plaza in front of the Imperial Palace, where the great red Communist flags whipped in the wind, I thought that the gifted, hysterical cook I remembered bleeding for the woes of China seemed somehow saner and more real than this Lao Pei, freshly numbered and neatly dressed in his criminal-cadre suit, marching along in the dust from one tar bucket to another.

RED GATES AND WATER DEVILS

MY WIFE'S Aunt Chin was only an in-law of the Yu family, like me, but where I had nothing more in the way of ancestry to offer than Virginia and Kentucky pioneer forebears, Aunt Chin traced her pure Manchu descent from an empress of China. In 1948, when I first knew Aunt Chin, I was a little afraid of her, and we didn't really become friendly until the summer of 1949 after I took up residence in the mansion. Aunt Chin, who was childless, had lived in her own suite of rooms there since her husband's death, some thirty years before. She had used no make-up in those thirty years, and she wore her heavy gray hair in a severe, straight-cut bob. The family respected her as much for the sharpness of her tongue as for the luster of her ancestry. They also considered her an authority on the history and lore of Peking and, in fact, she was an inexhaustible well of information—true, false, and absurd—about the city.

Aunt Chin lived with a companion, a mute who had never married and whom we called "Auntie Hu." She depended for her contact with outsiders on Aunt Chin, with whom she was able to communicate by some means too subtle for us to divine. When Auntie was unoccupied, her eyes followed Aunt Chin in whatever she was doing, watching for a moment where her services might be needed. I remember one autumn day before I had been formally introduced to them, coming upon the two old ladies in the garden, their arms outstretched, twirling in the fallen leaves. I retreated, so as not to spoil their fun.

Even after I had been formally introduced, they remained decidedly cool toward me until they discovered that I not only could play cards but, with Aimee, completed a foursome at bridge—a game dear to their hearts.

Aunt Chin kept cats, had asthma, and seldom left the house, or even her own rooms. Gambling and gossip were her only recreations, and after she and I became friends, my wife and I often played bridge or mah-jongg with her most of the night. Sometimes she would interrupt these sessions, and, an asthma cigarette between her lips, a row of ivory tiles or a deck of cards under her fingertips, she would talk.

"I bought that radio in 1937 to hear the hour-by-hour news of the Japanese invasion," she might say, indicating a cabinet against the wall, "and I haven't turned it on since. When the Japanese came south from Manchuria, they entered China through the gate in the Great Wall at Shanhaikwan. Our stupid generals left the gate open, and the dwarfs marched through. If we had closed that gate, the Japanese could *never* have got into China."

Aunt Chin shared with many old-fashioned Chinese an unquestioning faith in walls. Peking has always cherished this faith, and anyone living behind its massive walls, moats, and double gates cannot entirely escape a sense of security, however false. According to Aunt Chin, Peking fell to the Communists because someone opened the city gates and let them walk in. This was sufficient explanation in itself, but she would sometimes hint that she knew of another, and even more important, reason, and she would speak cryptically of the return of Peking's magic luck. Then she would change the subject, because she prided herself on understanding things of that sort, and felt that most other people—and especially foreigners—couldn't.

What she meant by her hints was, I learned, that the magic power—or, as she called it, "luck"—of the city was returning to make it once again the capital of China. For twenty-one years, despite its nine-hundred-year history as a seat of authority, it had been treated as an ordinary city by the Nationalists. Peking people have remained much the same through all their history. The Mongols, the Tartars, the Japanese—coups, counter-coups, and the fall of empires—have left little impression on them, and the arrival of the Communists, who were, after all, Chinese, seemed to them not so much a conquest as a change of regime. Aunt Chin, like all the rest of the family, cared little for the Communists, but like many others who were unenthusiastic about their regime, she felt a reluctant pride at the thought of the city's rising again to its proper place.

On the eve of the inauguration of the new Communist government—October 1, 1949, the day on which Peking was again to become the capital—Aunt Chin, her companion, and my wife, Aimee, and I were in Aunt Chin's rooms playing a game called *losung*, or Russian poker. "This government is putting on new clothes tomorrow," Aunt Chin said. "Do you think it will be much of a show?"

Aimee and I said that we thought it would be, and we described to her, as well as we could, the state of excitement the city was in. Schools, government offices, and labor organizations were all working on their contributions to the great parades that were to celebrate the occasion. Dance groups were practicing the Planting Dance, imported by the Communists from the provinces. Everyone was busy learning the songs of the New China, making costumes, and, because the demonstrations would last into the night, making lanterns.

The most spectacular preparations were centered on the walled plaza in front of the main gate—the Gate of Heavenly Peace—of the old Imperial Palace. From a balcony high up on the gate, Mao Tse-tung, all the officials of the new government, and the chiefs of those who are now known in China as "democratic personalities" (pro-Communist nonrevolutionaries) were to review the parades. Lesser "personalities" were to sit in grandstands built in front of the gate. There had formerly been groves of silk trees in the plaza, but these had been removed, and where they had stood, new concrete had been poured and flagstones laid. Floodlights had been mounted on steel towers all around the plaza. A famous pair of huge marble columns flanking the gate had been moved back to widen the road. Loudspeakers and microphones had been installed. The flaked red wall around the plaza had been repainted, and festoons of colored lights and banners—most of them bearing the legends "Long Live Chairman Mao Tse-tung!" and "Long Live the People's Republic of China!"— hung everywhere.

On the ramparts of the palace wall, at either side of the Gate of Heavenly Peace, stood four tall, slender poles, with an immense banner of gossamer red silk hanging from each of them. Under the eaves of the roofed, red-and-gold gate, nine ten-foot-high silk lanterns hung. In the middle of the plaza, workmen had drilled a hole as big as a well. It had turned out to be the foundation for a huge flagpole, on which now waved the flag of the People's Republic—one large and four small gold stars on a red field. The cosmic heart of Peking had been pierced with a flagpole. (Years later, the mausoleum of Mao Tse-tung was also to be built on this same sacrosanct axis.) The meaning of the flagpole was clear to all who lived in Peking. The old city had been struck its deathblow. For the time being, though, the gardens still flowered and the lacquer, gold and red, still gleamed on beam and door.

For months after its "liberation," Peking had gone about its business, and the Communists had directed their armies and administered their growing territories, while on the gate hung a peeling, two-story-high face of Chiang Kai-shek painted on gasoline tins that had been flattened and soldered together into a sheet. Now this was down, and for the first time in years the gate could be seen as its Ming architects had intended. When Mao's equally large picture had, inevitably, been put on display, it had been hung on the wall instead of on the gate.

After we had told all this to Aunt Chin, she merely advised us to take our umbrellas along if we were going to see the parades the next day. She pointed out that it had rained every time the new government held any sort of public demonstration, and she went on to explain why.

Two hundred years ago, she told us, the Ch'ien Lung Emperor traveled in disguise to the south of China by ship, and on the way a magic storm arose, during which the water devils, in the shapes of animals of the deep—crabs and fish of all kinds—rose up and held the ship fast, intending to sink it then and there. But the emperor, revealing his true identity to them, promised that if they let the ship proceed, they would all become government officials in a future incarnation, two hundred years later. This satisfied them, and they released the ship and sank down into the sea again. The storm subsided, and the emperor continued on his way, thinking no more of the incident. Nevertheless, an emperor's promise is sacred and may not be broken. Aunt Chin laughed. "They've all become Communist officials," she said. "But they're really water devils, and that's why it rains every time they come out."

Aimee and I looked severely at her, and she went on hurriedly, "There are many people in Peking who really believe this explains how the Communists came to power, but, of course, it's only a story. It never happened."

We had her now; we told her that after trying to pass off a story like that she would have to tell us what she thought the real reason was that, after so long, Peking's magic power had returned, and eventually she gave in.

The reason, she told us, lay at the Summer Palace. For

some years, this vast pleasure dome had been a public park and museum, its walls enclosing about four square miles of land, lake, and hills, northwest of Peking. I knew it well, because its former director had been my good friend and private pupil, studying English, and I had stayed there on holidays and weekends in 1947 and 1948. Aunt Chin did not know this, and I did not tell her. The main gate of the palace, she explained, faced east. There was a back gate, also, she said, facing north, which was closed from 1911, when the Manchu dynasty fell, until 1948, when, for some reason, it was suddenly opened by the palace administration.

The Western Hills and the great continental plateau to the north of the palace, she went on, were the reservoirs of the luck, or power, of Peking, which traditionally flowed down from the hills, entered the Summer Palace through the north gate, and went out the main, east gate on its way to Peking. When the back gate was closed in 1911, the decline of Peking had begun. When it was reopened in 1948, the luck had started to flow again. This hadn't helped the Nationalists, who were still in power, because their capital was Nanking. But the Communists had attached their fortunes to Peking's ascendant star, and they couldn't fail as long as the gate remained open.

Aunt Chin was serious about this story. It sprang from her belief in *feng-shui*, the magical science of Geomancy which Peking had depended on for centuries. Until recent times, no building in Peking was constructed without its builders' first making sure that it would conform to and magnify the natural luck inherent in the land it was to stand on.

Feng-shui is essentially a magic of terrain and direction, whose ancient practitioners were among the world's first surveyors and mapmakers. Every private home of any size in Peking has always had its own special *feng-shui*. In the Yu mansion, for instance, certain gates were kept closed to prevent luck from running out, and other gates were kept open to allow luck to run in. Unimportant outbuildings were built in the southwest corner of the property because southwest was the least lucky direction. Even the mansion's sewers conformed to its *feng-shui*.

When Aunt Chin had finished her story, I told her that I knew something she didn't about the opening of that gate at the Summer Palace. Aunt Chin wouldn't admit that any foreigner could know such a thing, so she refrained from asking me questions, but I noticed that she kept looking at me thoughtfully during the rest of the game.

At five o'clock the next day, Aimee and I left the house— without umbrellas—and set off in pedicabs for the Gate of Heavenly Peace. At that time, I was free to go about within the city walls as I liked. Later, especially after the outbreak of the Korean War, foreigners were put under restriction. In 1949, however, the government's attitude was not openly unfriendly to individual Americans, only to the policies of the United States government.

At the Avenue of Long Peace, we had to give up our pedicabs. The avenue, which crossed the plaza in front of the Gate of Heavenly Peace, was the parades' main line of march. When we got there, a tremendous procession of soldiers and horses, together with American trucks and tanks that had been captured from the Nationalists, was streaming along it.

As we struggled through the crowds, it began to grow dark. In about twenty minutes, we reached the western gate of the plaza and discovered that only those taking part in the demonstrations were being let through.

We stopped to rest against the bumper of a former American Army truck pulled up against the outside of the plaza wall, and resigned ourselves to seeing the parades from there and to not seeing the show inside the plaza at all. But the driver of the truck, hearing us, politely asked us to join him on top of his truck, where we could easily see over the wall. I went up first and pulled Aimee after me.

Sitting on the hard, high top of the cab, we looked into the great square, and found that we had a good, if distant, view of the Gate of Heavenly Peace. Beyond the southeast wall of the plaza we could see dimly the spires of churches, lights in the upper windows of the Wagons-Lits Hotel, and the black frame of the radio tower of the American consulate— landmarks of the old Foreign Legation Quarter.

Thousands of people were moving into the plaza and other thousands were filing out of it. The military parade had just ended, the driver told us, and the civilian one was about to begin. Floodlights illumined the road before the gate, where a workers' Western-style brass band, tooting and squeaking ineffectually against the noise of the crowd, was already marching. Colored lights outlined the gates and the wall, and the nine great lanterns swinging under the eaves of the gate glowed red. Standing beneath them, the rulers of China, spotlighted and clearly visible, moved their heads and arms. They looked oddly stiff and mechanical, like opera singers seen from the third balcony.

Another foreign-style band, sounding like an Edison recording of Sousa, marched through the plaza dressed in red-and-blue toy-soldier uniforms. The singers, who followed the bands, were better. They came in singing one of the many rousing folk songs adopted and reworded by the Communists: "Out of the East comes the sun, out of the East comes Mao Tse-tung." (Group singing was developed in the early years of the Sino-Japanese War, as a morale builder in free China, and since then it has been taken up with such general enthusiasm that there is some truth in the Communists' claim that it is the voice of modern China.)

As each group of marchers passed the center of the gate, they would chant, *"Mao Tse-tung Chuhsi, wan sui!"* ("Long live Chairman Mao Tse-tung!")

59

The voice of Mao would then answer, over the loudspeakers, "*Chung Hwa Jen Min Kung Ho Kuo, wan sui!*" ("Long live the People's Republic of China!")

The crowd and the marchers, throwing their arms up again and again, would roar back, "*Wan sui, wan sui*, WAN WAN SUI!" (Americans will remember this cheer as the "Banzai!"—literally meaning "Ten thousand years!"—of our recent Japanese enemies, who have taken so much of their language from the Chinese.)

Dancers—boys and girls dressed in scarves and turbans of colored silk—now entered the brightly lit area before the gate. Their faces were heavily powdered. Their lips were painted red and their eyebrows black. They marched ten abreast into the plaza, until four or five hundred of them filled the cleared space. Each dancer had a small drum suspended under each arm. Behind them, pulled by a group of boys, came their master drum, about five feet in diameter, mounted on wheels and surrounded by musicians holding cymbals, gongs, and temple blocks of resonant wood. A boy struck the great drum, and the dancers, in unison, took two swift steps forward, whirled, and began to strike in rhythm the drums under their arms—sometimes one, sometimes both drums simultaneously. The big drum beat out the dominant rhythm, and the temple blocks chattered fast, then slow, then fast again. The cymbals were struck on the first beat of every four, and the gongs on the third.

The dancers then began to move in the mincing, swaying gait of the Planting Dance, their heads rolling as if they were drunk. The steps were intricate, and were synchronized perfectly with the music. The dancers swayed right, whirled, took two steps backward, one step forward, with breathtaking precision.

Of course, no farmer ever danced such a dance during the planting or at any other season. I had seen the real Planting Dance eight months before, when it was first introduced into Peking, and it was a very dull dance. But government schools of dance, drama, and music had had their effect on the venerable steps of what Aunt Chin called "that vulgar country dancing."

Now, looking across the plaza, we could see lanterns bobbing along in the darkness beyond. They were of every size, shape, and color, and reminded me of the paper lanterns the Chinese use to represent the spirits of the dead on the Buddhist All Souls' Day. But these were not spirit lanterns. I didn't know what they were, but, watching them, and remembering our conversation with Aunt Chin, I imagined them somehow as the returned power of Peking flowing down from the Western Hills through the opened back gate of the Summer Palace.

Some of the lanterns were made in the shapes of Chinese characters signifying congratulation, happiness, or long life; others were the red stars of communism, or hammer-and-sickles. Many of the shapes were meaningless to me. We saw a great number of these carried into the plaza on bamboo poles of varying lengths. Suddenly the bearers converged and fitted their lanterns together above their heads, to form a huge fiery ship—the Chinese ship of state—riding on glowing blue-green waves.

Another group of marchers swung their lanterns together as they entered the plaza, and formed a luminous red replica of the Gate of Heavenly Peace. Other groups carried lanterns that, fitted together, made pagodas, flags, battleships, and tanks, and the continuing chant of "*Mao Tse-tung, wan sui, wan sui*, WAN WAN SUI!" mingled with the sounds of cymbals, trumpets, and drums rolling over the plaza and out across the old Forbidden City.

Soon fireworks began to go up, exploding high over the heads of the marchers and the watching crowds. Aimee and I sat three hours on the roof of the truck before we at last got down and pushed our way to a quieter street, where we found pedicabs, and then, passing still more parading groups, made our way home.

We found Aunt Chin and Auntie Hu sitting under a shaded light on a veranda that overlooked the garden, and watching the last of the fireworks bursting in the sky. We joined them, and drank tea and ate steamed jujube corn bread while Aunt Chin chatted. She had been to the end of the street and had seen parts of the parades pass by, and groups of dancers stopping to perform. "I never saw anything like it," she said. "All that singing about Mao Tse-tung and the people! You'd think nobody ever heard of people before! And what kind of farmers were those dancers?"

I explained that they weren't supposed to be real farmers, and she turned on me. "Whatever they are," she said, "they wouldn't be tramping our streets singing about the people at the top of their voices if someone at the Summer Palace hadn't opened the gate *you* were living in."

So my story of the gate was out. Aunt Chin, I surmised, had been at the telephone talking to friends and the servants of friends until she tracked it down, and now that she had finally given in to her curiosity, I had no objection to telling her the whole of the story. The gate in question was in the older part of the Summer Palace. When I first saw it, in 1947, I told Aunt Chin, it was in bad repair. An apartment in its upper story had at one time been luxuriously furnished and had been a retreat for Ch'ien Lung's mother, who liked to sit there and absorb merit by watching pilgrims pass along the road to the temples of the Western Hills.

Aunt Chin sniffed. "She was a very fine, devout woman," she said, "and one of my ancestors."

The whole upper floor, I went on, was glassed in, and faced open countryside on the north and the pine-shrouded hills of the Summer Palace on the south. I had liked it at once. The director had already promised to give me, in lieu of a fee for his lessons, a place of my own in the palace where I could spend holidays and weekends. So far, he hadn't managed it, because the many empty villas scattered through the grounds were spoken for. The grandest of these was reserved for Chiang Kai-shek, who since the defeat of Japan had spent only three days there. The old imperial living quarters had been turned into museums or leased as restaurants and summer hotels. Until I saw the apartment in the gate, I had found nothing for my own use.

At first, because of the state the place was in, the director was doubtful about letting me live there, but eventually he caught my enthusiasm and decided that it would be a worthwhile project to restore the gate to something like its original grandeur. He had it repainted a glittering Chinese red, and furnished it from the inexhaustible palace warehouses. The area around it was cleared of weeds and of many years' accumulation of dirt and fallen leaves. Even a few of the ancient flower plots were replanted. The barbed wire that had been strung outside the gate was removed, and so were the locks and seals that had been on it for almost forty years. When the whole place was in order, I moved in, and because a gatekeeper and an assistant gatekeeper had been directed to attend to my needs and to watch the gate now that it was no longer barred, my friend decided that the gate might as well be opened to the public.

Like my predecessor, the Mother Empress, I enjoyed watching the people go by. If, in these modern, disbelieving times, there were fewer pilgrims passing along the road, at least there were more tourists.

When the Communists took over the Summer Palace, along with Peking, they got my gate, too. I never went back to it except to pass through it as a tourist myself. The director retired to Peking, and the new palace administration left the gate as they had found it, open to the public. The upper story, where I had lived, was closed with the furnishings still in it.

Aunt Chin listened with her mouth open through most of

my story. "The fate of Peking determined by a foreigner!" she cried when I had finished. "The fate of all China ordained by my nephew-in-law!"

She sat for a while thinking, and several times she appeared about to speak in astonishment or outrage. I knew it must seem to her inconceivably presumptuous of me to have interfered, however inadvertently, with the destiny of China—to have restored the magic power to Peking and at the same time to have brought the dancing farmers, who were not farmers, into the streets.

In the end, she kept her own counsel. Aimee and I sat sipping our lukewarm tea in silence, and finally Aunt Chin said abruptly that she was going to bed. She and her companion stood up, and went down from the veranda into the garden. I called a good night to them, and Aunt Chin stopped and looked at me. "Good night," she said.

She came back a few steps, and I saw that she appeared tired, and perhaps puzzled, but no longer angry. "I know you're not really to blame," she said, and then she and her companion disappeared among the trees and rocks.

THE SEA OF WISDOM

I LAY AWAKE for some time that night thinking of the Summer Palace and my involvement with it, which had been far deeper than I cared to let Aunt Chin know. This palace lay a few miles outside of Peking near Tsinghwa University. It had been built by the Empress Dowager, T'su Hsi, at the end of the nineteenth century as her private retreat. Years in the building, it cost a sum so huge that, to this day, both Chinese and Western historians talk about it in tones of outrage, unwilling to forgive her for diverting the funds originally earmarked to create a Chinese navy. They do not see that this navy, had it been built, today would be lying at the bottom of the China Sea, sunk on its first encounter with a foreign power, while the empress's extravagance still stands, a delight to all who see it and, before the revolution when it was briefly my home, a very special delight to me.

Its grounds, open to the public during the day, were closed by sundown, and, after I had my own residence in the palace, it was then that I most liked being there. On warm moonlit nights my friends and I would embark upon the lake aboard my own "picture boat" complete with an oarsman, roof, table, benches, and whatever food and drink we had brought.

Sometimes we waited, while the oarsman slept, for the first rays of sunrise to touch the curved rooftops of the Sea of Wisdom, a mysterious and imposing rectangular two-story building straddling the hill's topmost ridge, which had always intrigued me and would have intrigued Aunt Chin, too, had I told her the story. Built in the eighteenth century and pre-dating the Empress Dowager's construction, this "sea" above the "mountain" was covered in yellow- and green-glazed tiles, each containing a niche in which sat a glazed-tile Buddha. Thousands of Buddhas sat in thousands of niches the height and breadth of the building. Some heads were missing; in 1900 the occupying Western forces, bored and angry amidst so much beauty, had used them for target practice.

I would like to have told Aunt Chin, if I had dared, the story of the Sea of Wisdom and the opening of the three red lacquer double doors set within marble arches in the south facade of the building. Barred from within by great wooden beams, the building could only be entered by a small door on its narrow east end. This door was clasped shut by a jumble of rusty Chinese locks hanging along the opening between its panels. A multitude of paper strips bearing writing and seals were pasted across the opening. These had been put up by every succeeding palace administration since the fall of the dynasty in 1911, attesting that the authorities had found the building locked and had left it that way.

Sitting at the very top of the hill dominating the Summer Palace, the Sea of Wisdom was clearly the most important building there, and I wondered what secret it contained. The director, whom I questioned one afternoon, knew nothing about the building's contents. Nor did his aide, who left and returned with the information that an old man in the nearby village who worked in the palace during the last days of the dynasty had heard—just heard, mind you—that gold might be inside. The director decided then and there to open the building and invited me to be present.

On a sunny morning a few days later, members of the palace staff, the director, and I gathered before the door in the east wall of the Sea of Wisdom. One of the workmen carried a bunch of rusty Chinese keys, which he proceeded to apply to the locks while the director broke the paper seals one by one. When the last seal had been broken and the last lock opened—I was mildly surprised to see that a key existed for every lock—the director stepped back and a workman pulled open the squeaking panels.

In the bright sunlight the utter blackness within was disquieting. The smell of must swelled out, and I wondered if the building might be a tomb. For a moment no one moved, and then one of the workmen stepped inside and disappeared into what I now thought might better be called the "Sea of Darkness." In a short while we heard the sound of a heavy wooden bolt being drawn back, and then the dowels of the central doors beginning to turn in their wooden sockets. As the doors parted, I saw a sliver of blinding light shoot through the darkness to reveal a golden Buddha soaring two stories high almost to the ceiling. When opened, the flanking doors exposed two more golden Buddhas to the left and right. In the bright sunlight with all the doors opened, these Buddhas symbolizing the Past, Present, and Future, each on a shoulder-high marble pedestal, created a dazzling effect. The sea of darkness had become a sea of golden light.

The director decided to leave the building open so the public might also see the Buddhas, which on closer inspection proved to date from the eighteenth century, were made of bronze, and in the Tibetan style. No one seemed to mind that we had not found gold of a more portable nature.

Less than a year later, just before the palace fell to the conquering Communist armies and before I fled to the seeming safety within the mighty walls of Peking, the director reclosed the Sea of Wisdom. It was still closed when, months later, after the siege had ended and the Communists were in power, I was able to revisit the palaces that had so recently been mine. An attendant I knew would not speak to me until he had led me to a place where no one could see us. There, he told me that the director had been taken away and warned me not to mention his name, go to my rooms over the north gate, or ever reveal that I had once lived there.

I visited the Summer Palace only a few more times and always found the doors of the Sea of Wisdom closed. On my final visit to the building I noticed on its side door new paper seals and one shiny Western-style padlock replacing all the old. Had she known, I shudder to imagine what new ills Aunt Chin might suppose my meddling had brought upon China.

SILVER PINS AND
BLOOD-RED SKIRTS

THE YU FAMILY loved the garden more than any other part of their establishment. I, too, learned to appreciate the garden. Unlike a Japanese garden, which is made chiefly to be looked at, a Chinese one is meant to be walked in. It is a private landscape of careful deceptions, a deliberate reminder of those wet black-and-green mountains, the home of immortals and monkeys, found in Chinese paintings. In it, the wise man is able to see the world of dust and bustle as he thinks it should be seen—at a distance, and through leaves.

I often walked in the garden of my wife's home, and if I gathered no wisdom, at least I enjoyed the tree-shaded pebble paths, the bamboo groves (of which the family was particularly proud, because bamboo is rare in North China), and the cool blackness of the rock grottoes. At the time I lived there, the hydraulic mechanism installed to pump water from the well into the garden's two pools had gone hopelessly out of repair. When the family holdings lost their value, Elder Brother, in his effort to economize, had tried to raise pigs in one of the pools, but they never seemed to thrive there, and after the night when one of them got out and had to be cornered, squealing and kicking, in the Pavilion of Harmonious Virtues, Elder Brother abandoned the project.

Sometimes, in the summer of 1949, Aimee and I would sit on porcelain stools in the Pavilion of Harmonious Virtues, eating watermelon that had been cooled in a cage at the bottom of the well, and she would point out to me the distant peak of Mount T'ai—simulated there in the garden—or a nearer mountain range, in which we could see the fortress gate of the Western Pass. All this was no more than one or two hundred feet away from us, and I knew that I would have to bend my head to pass through the mighty Western Gate, and that I could climb to the top of Mount T'ai in about twenty seconds by way of a set of concealed stone steps on its far side. But sometimes, listening to Aimee as she showed me such things, I could see the garden as the artist who designed it over four hundred years ago intended it should be seen—as an immensity of space and distant mountains.

The Pavilion of Harmonious Virtues, from which I was best able to see the illusions, stood in the center of the garden. Four slender wooden posts, riddled by dry rot, held up the pavilion's heavy tile roof and elaborately bracketed eaves, and though the whole structure tilted slightly, it was able to maintain an equilibrium that defied time and age. Nevertheless, by the spring of 1950, the pavilion's list toward the southwest (the malevolent direction) had become so noticeable that the family took it to be a bad omen.

There was another omen in the garden that spring. For the first time in memory, the peach, plum, and cherry trees there bloomed at the same time, and the family, convinced that this had some deep significance, eventually decided it must be the garden's way of saying farewell. Faced with a set of new and fiercer taxes, they had begun to concede defeat in their attempt to hold together, and were realizing that in a matter of months the mansion would have to be given up and the family scattered. So, although tempers had recently been short and arguments frequent, for the brief time of the garden's blooming the family spoke quietly, with elegance and ease, in the way I imagined they had spoken long before. The complaints, the postures of despair, the threats of suicide or of death by starvation were set aside, and the family did what for them, that spring, was a very surprising thing. They decided to have a tea in the extravagantly blooming garden.

The tea, in keeping with the spring's lavishness, turned out to be a far larger affair than the family had at first anticipated. It became, in fact, a costume ball, arranged and paid for by Hetta Empson. Fond of the garden as we were, she was, if possible, even fonder. She would come just to sit there on moonlit nights in summer. In the autumn, she would carry away great bunches of chrysanthemums from the garden, and when the first snow fell she was sure to appear, eager to see the whitened rocks and trees. It was no wonder, then, that the unnatural splendor of the garden that spring inspired her. She decided that all Peking, or at least all the people, Chinese and foreign, that she—and I—knew in Peking, should have an opportunity to see it. And what better way could there be to arrange this than to give a costume party on the night of the first full moon? Already softened by the garden's saying farewell, the family gave their consent, and looked on the affair as their way of saying farewell, in turn, to the garden.

When the party was decided on, there were only a few days left before the full moon. Hetta got to work. She sent out invitations; she hired a dance band from Scatter When the Rain Comes, one of Peking's few remaining nightclubs; she sent her own servants to help take up the carpets and move most of the furniture out of the Hall of Ancient Pines, which had a tile floor and tile veranda, and would make an excellent place to dance; and she arranged to have lanterns hung throughout the garden.

The family's chief contribution to the party was to tell all those friends whom they had intended to invite to a tea that, because there would soon be a full moon, and because the garden would be lit by lanterns on that night, the flowers would probably look very pretty, and they were invited to come and look at them. In addition, Elder Brother called in the family's electrician, who tapped the city electric lines that ran just outside the garden wall. He came the night before the party and, with a few lengths of wire strung over the wall and carefully concealed, ensured abundant and free electricity. I was surprised to discover that, despite its past great wealth, the family had been lighting the garden in just that way for years.

On the night of the party, the huge moon that appeared over the wall of the garden was first of an ominous orange color and then, as it rose higher, a pale, watery yellow. When the lanterns were turned on, the garden looked very pretty, but they could not completely dispel the uneasy influence of that sickly moonlight, and the garden seemed not at all the one with which I had become familiar.

From all parts of the city, the guests began to arrive, emerging from one pedicab after another, their varied costumes greatly amusing the gateman. After some thirty or forty had come, I began to detect trends in the choice of costume. Most of the Europeans came as traditional Chinese—mandarin officials, empresses, or singsong girls. The younger Chinese came as Indians, in saris and turbans, and the Indians (largely exchange students) came as Communists, in Party "cadre uniforms." Being an American, I was, perhaps, part of the odd pattern, wearing a Japanese kimono and a long black wig.

There were costumes outside these major categories. Aimee, in a red skirt, wearing paper roses in her hair and carrying a tambourine, was a Spanish gypsy, and there was the inevitable sprinkling of sheeted Arabs. Hetta came as Scheherazade, in a sort of breastplate of colored beads that caused a certain amount of controlled giggling among the younger Chinese women.

The young and wealthy Eugene Chiang wore an unbelievable pink tweed business suit and a turban made (so he told us) of nine yards of pink chiffon. Eugene loved to dance. He even danced through the siege of Peking. He came with his friend Ma Shih-rung (we called him Mushroom with no disrespect), the last male of an old Manchu family, who lived alone with his sister in a huge moldering mansion in the North City. His sister should have been the last empress of China. Passed over because of a slight mental disorder and having one leg shorter than the other, she did not attend the party.

Walter Brown, an American teacher costumed as a harem keeper, arrived with the elegant Charlotte Horstmann, born in Peking of a Chinese mandarin father and a German mother. She lived in a beautiful house on Sweet Water Well Lane, owned an antique shop in the lobby of the Peking Hotel, and came as a Manchu princess in an embroidered gown and kingfisher feather crown. We expected no less.

Bob Winter, a tall, amusing man, and one of the oldest American residents of Peking, came as Fu Manchu with a string tied under his nose for a mildly sinister effect. He escorted the legendary and often-married Magdelene Grant, then still spoken of as the most beautiful woman on the China coast. Born in Java of Dutch parents, she had come to China in the thirties while on her honeymoon with a Dutch businessman twice her age. At dock-side in Shanghai she is reported to have expressed great surprise on being informed that her husband was nowhere to be found, apparently having fallen overboard sometime during the voyage. She wore a hoop skirt, had hidden her gold red hair under a white wig, and looked like nothing I had ever seen.

An English diplomat dressed as a mandarin said to me about another guest, attired as a Mongolian princess, complete with oiled black hair encrusted with coral and turquoise, and arranged over a frame of what looked like horns, "My God! What a fabulous costume."

"That's not a costume," I answered. "She really is a Mongolian princess."

"Well," said the diplomat, much intrigued, "I think I'll ask her to dance," and he did. I hadn't the heart to tell him that the Mongolian princess was really a Mongolian prince.

But despite individual deficiencies or excesses, the guests looked pleasantly exotic strolling in the garden or in the Hall of Ancient Pines, tripping over their hems and trailing their veils in polkas, Lambeth walks, and congas. Since the revolution, the Lambeth walk and the conga had become the two most popular Western dances in Peking, the non-Communist population and foreigners hoping that they looked like the kind of healthy, mass-participation dances of which the Communists would be apt to approve. (A conga line does, in fact, bear a surprising resemblance to the Planting Dance, and the Lambeth walk is similar to the Russian style of ballroom dancing then being introduced in Peking, in which couples line up against one wall and, to a kind of military-waltz rhythm, stride purposefully, arm in arm, to the opposite wall, turn around, and, chins outthrust, stride back again.)

When the orchestra wasn't playing "progressive" music for these dances, it stuck to snappy, surefire pieces like "Lady of Spain," "I Dreamt That I Dwelt in Marble Halls," and "China Night." The last is a Japanese song that was banned during the first years of the American occupation of Japan on the ground that it smacked of Japanese imperialism, although, with Chinese words, it had been an immense success in China during the Japanese occupation and, after the war, was one of the few remaining bits of evidence that the Japanese had ever been there. I have heard that there is also an American version of the song, mysteriously entitled "Truly Luly Lulu."

While the music played, servants passed trays of drinks—vodka, and fruit juice, and the standard cocktails. For the confirmed drinkers, there was plenty of Chinese *pai gar*, one of the world's more potent drinks. It looks like gin, is drunk warm, and leaves the drinker with a breath like automobile exhaust. We also had the gentler Chinese yellow rice wine, which is warmed before drinking, too, and tastes to me like straw, although I've known people who claimed it to be very like sherry. Using chopsticks two feet long, the guests grilled strips of lamb over charcoal braziers set up in the garden, and ate them, Mongolian fashion, with chopped leeks, ginger, and vinegar. Later, the young man in the pink turban sang what was then a new song, beginning, "I want to get you on a slow boat to China." It was not a success, but a variant—"I want to get myself on a fast boat leaving China"—occurred simultaneously to a number of people, and was. There was a good deal of laughter, and in the midst of it a late guest dressed as Yang Kuei-fei, the most beautiful empress in Chinese history, came up to me. "Who rates the guard of honor?" she asked, with a strong American accent.

"What guard of honor?" I asked.

"Why, those soldiers with guns at the front gate," she said.

I told her that she must have seen some of the guests, in costume, but I had seen no one with a gun, so I excused myself, and found Aimee and called her aside. "Do you know anything about soldiers at the gate?" I asked. She looked surprised, and I said, "They may be only guests, but we'd better go and see."

When Aimee and I got to the main gate, we found that there were indeed two soldiers there, one on each side of the gate. Hand grenades hung at their belts, and each carried an obviously real gun with bayonet attached. Aimee rattled her tambourine at them. "Why are you standing here?" she demanded.

Just then the gateman ran up from the direction of the garden. "I've been trying to find you," he said to Aimee. "These soldiers came here a while ago, and when I ask them what they want they won't answer. Look." He turned and shouted to them. "What do you want? Why are you standing here?" They made no response. "You see?" he said, turning back to Aimee.

"Perhaps there's someone outside who's in charge of them," she said. She started through the gate, but the soldiers suddenly lowered their guns to block her. "Can't I even go out of my own house?" she cried furiously, and just then a pedicab pulled up in front of the gate and a "mandarin" in full court dress—still another late arrival—emerged. He lifted a painted eyebrow at the sight of the soldiers, who had resumed their positions and were staring straight ahead like hitching posts, and walked between them without hindrance. Evidently the gate could be used in one direction only.

Aimee then went off to find Elder Brother while I escorted the new guest to the garden. Coming into it out of the comparative darkness of the courtyards we had passed through on the way was a shock. The fruit-tree blossoms, reflecting the orange and blue lights of the lanterns, hung like gauze veils receding, one behind another, into the remote corners of the garden. A wind had sprung up, and the petals, already past their prime, were falling everywhere, thick and glittering, while people in shining red brocades and crowns of feathers and jewels strolled to the sound of still another conga.

I didn't like it. I still could not recognize the garden—it might as well have been a Chinese garden in Burbank or Rio de Janeiro—and I felt, now, that I did not know, or could not recognize, the people. All of them were strangers to me and to the place. I was glad that the party was none of my doing and that although I lived in the house, I was, at the moment, only another guest.

I took leave of my mandarin as soon as I could, and went back through the quiet courtyards to the rooms occupied by old Aunt Chin. She was there, an asthma cigarette drooping from her lips, playing solitaire. She looked up when I entered. The wind had suddenly become much stronger, and some of her cards fluttered to the floor. I picked them up and asked her if she wanted me to close her windows.

"What are you?" she asked sharply, pointing to my costume. "A devil from the underworld? Well, if you have human hands, you might as well close the windows. You ghosts and devils in the garden are raising quite a wind." Under ordinary circumstances, she might have annoyed me—she was trying to—but just then I was too uneasy and depressed to answer her. "Some soldiers are here," I told her as I closed the windows. "They're going to arrest us all."

"Are they?" she said calmly. She began to gather up her cards, which had worked out in a winning game; Aunt Chin always won at cards, even when she played against herself. "I am not surprised at that. You are all impostors," she said, and I could see that she was serious. "You know nothing of the history of China, and yet you are trying to imitate the illustrious prodigals of antiquity, who also went down to destruction." She slapped the cards onto the table and, her head swaying, chanted what I took to be part of a poem: "Golden pendants and silver pins are smashed, and blood-red skirts are stained with wine!" She stopped abruptly, and then spoke again. "That is how the great have always perished," she said. "Their sins turned day to night and their follies opened the gates of Hell, but they lived boldly and, when the time came, died boldly, too. You out there in the garden, celebrating your own end, are nothing like them, however you may dress." Clearly, Aunt Chin misunderstood the purposes of costume parties, but she refused to be interrupted. "With the rebel armies at the gates of the palace, the last Ming emperor cut down all his concubines, daughters, and even the empress with his own sword before he hung himself," she said. "In the confusion, he failed to decapitate the empress, cutting off one of her arms instead. Disgraced at finding herself still alive, the empress threw herself into a garden well and drowned. It was the only virtuous thing to do. And the ancients! When *their* time came, they dressed in pearled robes and crowns of jade, and were murdered in palaces of sandalwood and cassia so huge the smoke of their burning hung over the whole land. They were phoenixes and dragons, and compared to them you poor imitators are no more than the ghosts of butterflies and crickets."

She fell silent, and I knew it would be useless to explain or argue with her. Besides, I felt that she had shown her usual uncanny knack for hitting the nail on the head no matter how wrong her premise might be. So, removing my wig, I sat down opposite her at the table. And, still in silence, she dealt a hand of rummy, and we played.

Aunt Chin won the first round, and we were starting on a second when Aimee came in. "So this is where you are," she said. "It's terrible. Elder Brother tried to go out and they wouldn't let him, and some of the guests wanted to go home and they wouldn't let them. Someone finally telephoned the police station, and they told us they're deciding what to do about us. They say we're breaking the law by holding a private meeting. They've never heard of a costume party, of course."

I remembered that there is no word in Chinese for party. A few young moderns I knew used the Chinese transliteration, "*p'a-t'i*," but most people simply said "*k'ai-hui*," which means "hold a meeting"—and that was exactly what we had no permit for. Aimee went on, "And now we don't know what to do. No one is allowed to leave until the police make up their minds, and I think a storm is coming. The moon is still out, but it's such a strange color."

"There's going to be a dust storm," Aunt Chin said. "I could have told you that this morning, if you'd asked me. Of course, no one around here ever gets up early enough to see the sunrise. All the signs were right, and this is the season. The moon looks strange because of the dust in the air."

Aimee went back to the garden, but as there was nothing I could do about the police or the coming storm, I stayed where I was.

Aunt Chin won the next round, too, and by the time we were well into the third, the wind was making a whistling sound, the latticed, paper-covered windows rattled and popped, and I had begun to feel fine grit between my teeth. I was just beginning to think I had better go back to the party when Aimee returned.

She told us that the police had telephoned and said that everyone could go. The guards had been called away from the gate, and the guests were now leaving. The police had indicated that they were coming around themselves, within the next hour, to see what was going on here.

Surrendering an excellent hand, I put my wig back on and followed Aimee through the windy courtyards to the garden, to say good-bye to the remaining guests. I could hear and feel the dust whispering underfoot as we went. In the garden, the trees had been blown almost bare, and fallen petals swirled in the shadows cast by the swinging lanterns. The members of the orchestra, carrying their black instrument cases, were just leaving. Scheherazade and a small group who had stayed to the end with her were wading through a pile of petals, clutching their costumes about them and carrying broken headdresses. From the veranda of the Hall of Ancient Pines, Aimee and I waved to them, and then we went inside the hall. There Elder Brother and several of Aimee's sisters joined us, and we waited for the arrival of the police. The family considered my presence necessary because so many of the foreign guests had been acquaintances of mine but strangers to the family, and it was assumed that questions would be asked about them.

The dust was now everywhere in the tightly closed hall, seeping in between windows and their frames, and under the door. I took off my wig once more and draped it over the back of a chair. Presently, someone turned off the garden lanterns, and we continued to sit in the dimly lit room, surrounded by the sound of the wind, until at last we saw the Communist police picking their way by flashlight through the crumbling garden.

Elder Brother went to meet them, and ushered two officials into the hall. An underling stayed outside. The officials sat down, and immediately one of them jumped up again, striking out at something behind him. He had sat on the chair with my wig hanging on it, and I suppose the wind had blown the hair against his neck. He was given another seat, which he accepted suspiciously, and Third Sister brought cups of hot tea, which neither policeman would drink. Another sister offered them cigarettes, which they refused. "Will you please show us where you held this dance meeting?" one of them asked. His use of the word "dance" seemed to indicate that the police had already come a long way toward our explanation of the evening's activity.

"Here," Elder Brother answered. "In this room and in the garden."

The police looked around in surprise at the dusty room. Plainly it was hard for them to believe that we could have held a party in it.

"But all those people in the expensive clothes—do you mean they came *here*?" the other man asked.

Elder Brother pointed to the overflowing ashtrays and to the scattering of empty glasses on window sills and on the arms of a few chairs and sofas backed against the walls. Most of the litter had been left on a buffet on the veranda, and had been carried away by the servants when the wind began to rise, but the remainder was evidence enough, and the police settled down to giving us a lecture.

We ought to be ashamed of ourselves, they told us, for causing them so much anxiety. What had we expected them to think, they asked peevishly, when flocks of pedicabs began to pass their station at the end of the street, all coming in this direction and all filled with strangely dressed people? The men they sent to investigate had been further astounded to hear loud foreign music and the sound of laughter wafting over the walls. We must admit that we had behaved very peculiarly, they said, and couldn't we at least have let the police know what we were doing?

Elder Brother explained politely that it had been a moon-and-flower-viewing party, and that, because the moon and the flowers couldn't wait, we had been in such a rush to hold the party that we had completely overlooked the important matter of informing the People's Police of our innocent pleasures.

"Moonlight and flowers!" one of the policemen cried contemptuously. He brought out a sheaf of papers from his valise, saying that since we had failed to make a written request at the proper time for permission to hold a private meeting, we must do so now. We must do it before another minute passed, and we must also fill out a form listing the names of all the people who had attended our dance meeting.

Aimee and I did what we could with the form. I gave her as many names of foreign guests as I could recall, and she wrote them down, transliterated by their sounds into Chinese. It was unlikely that anyone could decipher them. In the meantime, Elder Brother wrote the request and a letter of apology for not having submitted it earlier.

He was just impressing his personal seal on the form and letters when, over the sound of the wind, we heard a loud creaking and cracking out in the garden, followed by a sound rather like that of an immense cabinet filled with thousands of dishes falling over. We all rushed to the windows just as the underling left on guard outside came bursting into the room.

"What happened? What happened?" the officers asked.

"I don't know," he said, getting as far away from the door as possible. "I don't know."

Elder Brother strode manfully out into the wild, dark night. "What's going on out here?" we heard him call, and through the door I saw him throw the switch that controlled all the lanterns strung in the trees. They flashed on, leaping about in the branches like fiery goblins, their paper coverings torn by the wind. The sudden illumination came as a complete surprise to the police, who gasped in unison.

Then we saw that the Pavilion of Harmonious Virtues had collapsed. Its roof tiles were scattered in all directions, and the roof itself lay half on, half off the stone terrace on which the pavilion had stood. We had just time to realize what had happened when, accompanied by sparks from the switch, all the lanterns went out again.

Elder Brother came back in. "It's lucky I had those lights put on a special fuse," he said. "I was expecting they might blow it."

"What about the pavilion?" one of the family asked. "Can we put it up again?"

"It doesn't matter," Elder Brother said. "We'll be losing the house soon anyway."

For a while, immersed in the behavior of the lights and the collapse of the pavilion, the rest of us had forgotten the police. Finally, one of them asked in an urgent whisper, "Is it safe to go back out through the garden?"

Elder Brother assured him that it was.

"Then we must be going," the other said, and both of them gathered up their papers. "We'll come back tomorrow."

Elder Brother led them out, and that was the last we saw of them. They never came back, and nothing more was said to us about our illegal meeting—the reason being, we surmised, that what they saw of it had struck them as such a miserable example of reactionary merrymaking that they decided not to risk the perils of the garden to investigate further.

When they had gone, that night, the family began to drift off to bed. Intending to follow, I first bent over to retrieve my hank of hair, which had slipped onto the floor. Lying beside it was a silver butterfly pin, crushed flat, its wings broken. Pins like it were on sale in all the junk-jewelry stalls in the Peking markets for about fifteen cents. Many of the guests had probably used them to hold their costumes together. But despite the fact that it was a very ordinary object, I found myself remembering the pin of Aunt Chin's poem, and the butterfly ghosts she had invoked, and I shuddered to think of the conclusions she would have drawn if she had found it. I picked it up and dropped it in the garden well on my way to bed. Unlike the Ming empress, who had, no doubt, made a very loud splash, my broken butterfly made no sound at all when it hit the water, but I felt I had done the right thing.

Aimee in 1950 wearing her famous dragon ear-
rings and performing a dance from a classical
Chinese opera at the old Asia Institute in New
York in 1951.

At the Summer Palace in 1948.

The Summer Palace in winter with the Sea of Wisdom at
the top of the Hill of Ten Thousand Years.

Upper floor of my apartment in the North Gate of the Summer Palace. John Blofeld, Walter Brown, Hetta Empson, Sir William Empson, and I. 1948.

John Blofeld, Walter Brown, myself, and Hetta Empson in the Summer Palace in 1948.

Yu Garden in snow.

Aimee in the Yu garden with a friend's child.

Eastern Study Library.

The Hall of Ancient Pines in the Yu garden, stones bordering an empty pool in the foreground.

Corridors connecting Yu family buildings.

Taking tea with Aimee in the Yu garden.

THE ANCESTORS

W<small>HEN OLD</small> Mr. Yu died, his name tablet, a plaque of carved wood about a foot high and four inches wide, joined the tablets of his dead wife, his parents, and his paternal grandparents and great-grandparents on a simple large altar that stood in the Yu mansion's main hall. Before it, the family performed daily rites, including the offering of food, wine, and incense.

These tablets were more than mementos of the dead; they were believed to be the dead, each containing a part of the dead person's spirit. They were made of cypress or Chinese juniper, and were unpainted and unstained, except that on some of them the name of the person had been painted rather than carved. The older ones, varying from four inches to a foot or so in height, were covered by cases of the same wood, which could simply be lifted off if one wished to see the tablet. Near the top of each case was a small opening of carved grillwork, through which, when the light entered from just the right angle, the upper part of the name tablet could be seen. Without their outer sheaths, the tablets were just straightforward-looking pieces of wood, but hidden behind their latticed windows they always gave me the feeling that they did contain some kind of presence, which knew when I was looking at it.

When my father-in-law's tablet was put on the altar, I was told that, by Chinese custom, it would be worshiped for three generations. Not until his last great-grandchild died might his and his wife's tablets be removed to the family's ancestral temple, where those of all the more remote Yu dead reposed. During his lifetime, Mr. Yu had faithfully worshiped the tablets of the three generations preceding his, but now his children were not obliged to continue to observe the rituals before the tablets of their great-great-grandparents, and they decided that these (now over a hundred years old) should be removed to the temple. I had never visited this temple, and I was curious to see it. As a matter of fact, it was quite unusual for a private Chinese family to have an ancestral temple at all, other than the one maintained in the house itself. In a large Chinese house these ancestral altars usually occupy a room in the northeast courtyard.

The temple was situated, I was told, on the shore of the northernmost of Peking's seven lakes. No tablets had been taken there for several decades. It had been the duty of old Mr. Yu to make periodic visits to it, but during his last years he had been too weak to do so, and the temple had fallen into disrepair, owing partly to the children's changing attitude toward ancestor worship and in a good measure to the dwindling of the family's funds during the troubled times.

As a matter of fact, none of the living members of the family seemed really to care about the ancestors, but they were compelled, by pride and the wish to exercise good faith, to fulfill the minimum terms of the contract that bound the living to the dead. They were determined that if Great-Grandfather Yu had died, as he had, in the belief that he would be honored and remembered according to custom, their generation, at least, would not be the one to let the rituals lapse. I think it was pretty much understood, however, that theirs was to be the last generation responsible to the ancestors; although the contract had not yet been broken, notice was being served.

One bright morning in early summer, Aimee told me she would take me to see the ancestral temple that afternoon if I cared to go. She wanted to visit it and bring back to the family a report on its condition, though actually it wasn't necessary to see it to know that it would need repairs. Any Chinese building left untended for even a few years needs extensive repairs, yet somehow, when none are forthcoming, it is likely to manage to go on standing for centuries.

After lunch that day, Aimee called a pair of pedicabs and gave me a string of jangling brass keys to carry, saying they were the keys to the temple. Aimee and I were lucky to get fairly fast pedicabs, and after we had left the narrow street on which the mansion gate opened, we sailed north on the great street running north and south through the west side of the city. In less than fifteen minutes, we reached the point where the street turned westward. Abandoning it there, our pedicabs continued north, bumping through a labyrinth of dusty alleys and streets that became increasingly narrow. Aimee, who was in the lead pedicab, wrapped a scarf around her hair and the lower half of her face.

Suddenly, after crossing a low stone bridge, the street we were on widened, and we found ourselves going along the shore of a lake, on the far side of which rose the gray brick north wall of the city. We went on around the lake, and as we approached the wall, its huge slope seemed to rise higher and higher, until it blocked out all the northern sky. Reaching the base of the wall, our pedicabs turned east onto a path that ran between it and the lake.

This part of the city interested me, although I had never seen it before. Now I realized, as we crossed another stone bridge, that it was here that the cold, clean water from the Jade Fountain—a natural spring about ten miles northwest of Peking—entered the city. The Fountain is the main source of water for all the canals and moats and decorative lakes of Peking (the drinking water comes from other sources), and its water flows through these and, far underground, through the city's ancient stone sewers, to empty, at last, dark brown and thick as soup, into a ditch outside the southwest wall.

At that time, the Communists were already boasting that because of their repairs of the countless water gates and sluices in the old hydraulic system, and because of their dredging of the lakes and canals, Peking's water changed completely every four days. The lakes and moats did seem cleaner, although I had no way of knowing whether any particular patch of water I happened to be looking at was more than four days old. Certainly this water in Peking's northernmost lake was the cleanest I had seen. Fresh from the countryside, and still smelling of moss and lichen, the spring water boiled into the city through an iron grille in the base of the wall and, forming deep black whirlpools, entered the lake under the bridge our pedicabs had just crossed.

Presently, our road narrowed to pass between the city wall and the wall of a compound built on a piece of land jutting out into the lake. The pedicab men threw on their brakes, and we came to a halt on the narrowest part of the road, before a dilapidated roofed gate in the compound wall. Aimee asked me to give her the keys, and while I paid the pedicab men, she opened the gate.

Entering most Chinese gates, one can see only walls and more walls, but when I went through this one, I found myself with an unobstructed view of the lake. To my right, facing south on a raised terrace, stood a large temple in great disrepair and wearing an air of complete abandonment. "That's our temple," Aimee said.

We walked to the front of it and onto a large tiled terrace, badly pitted and overgrown with grass. Aimee turned and studied the temple. Its eaves had rotted away in a number of places, leaving great holes, and its windows—latticed in a design of interlocked swastikas, the Buddhist symbol of eternity—looked as if cannon balls had been shot through them. Everywhere around the base of the building lay bits of decayed wood and broken roof tiles. Aimee sighed. "It certainly needs repairs," she said. "I can remember when we used to come here on summer nights, years ago when Mama was still alive, to watch the moon and feel the lake breeze. We drank wine and told stories and sang songs, and we didn't go home until the moon went down." She thought awhile, and then added, "During a siege, it's very safe here, because shells high enough to pass over the city wall will also pass over this temple."

We tried the main double doors. Though there were no visible locks on them, they would not open, seeming to be held shut by some kind of bar inside the temple. But one of the smaller doors, alongside these, had a lock of the kind that Westerners sometimes call a "Chinese puzzle lock." It looks like an ordinary Chinese lock, but there are two keys to it, and it must be unlocked twice. Aimee, applying herself to this one—there is a special knack to undoing these locks—mastered it in a short time. Then she pushed the door open on its creaking wooden hinges, and we stepped into the temple through a shower of dust.

My first impression was of funereal chaos. A tiered altar, rising to the ceiling and covering almost the whole of the north wall, was crowded to overflowing with spirit tablets hung with dusty cobwebs and leaning giddily in all directions. Many lay on their sides or had fallen to lower tiers and had come to rest upside down. The altar looked as if it had been shaken by an earthquake. On a long table stood a number of sacrificial vessels—incense burners, candlesticks, vases, and other receptacles—but few even of these were upright. Aimee said that the wind, blowing through the broken windows, was responsible for the disorder.

Standing against the walls were several large black-and-red lacquered chests covered with debris—fragments of lanterns and staffs, dismembered Buddhist statuary, stringless harps, and a great number of brass bells. Tatters of what had once been a brocade canopy hung from the ceiling, and the floor was covered with a thick gray-yellow carpet of dust that puffed up underfoot in sluggish clouds whenever we moved, and then settled quickly.

I asked Aimee what the chests contained, and by way of answer she handed me the keys. While she busied herself lighting incense on the altar table, I tried key after key in the lock of the nearest chest until I found the right one, and then, after clearing away pieces of the plaster halo of one of the statues, a broken plaster arm, and some bells, lifted the lid. The chest was packed to the brim with tightly rolled red scrolls, each marked with a name written in black on a strip of gold paper. I lifted out a scroll and, unfastening the bone clasp, allowed it to unroll onto the floor.

The scroll was an ancestor's portrait, painted on silk. The silk had once been white, I knew, but had dulled to a smoky brown background for the still bright golds, reds, and blues of the picture, which was that of a very stern old man who resembled Aimee's elder brother and, for that matter, Aimee herself. The man was dressed in full mandarin costume and sat in a thronelike chair on a strip of intricately patterned carpet. The picture was minutely detailed. Even the hairs in the old man's sable hat were painted with individual brush strokes.

There were at least two hundred scrolls in the chest. Aimee had come over, and I asked her if all the chests were filled with paintings. She answered that probably most of them were. "Why don't you sell them, then, since the family needs money?" I asked.

Aimee laughed. "Who wants pictures of someone else's ancestors? They aren't worth anything, except sometimes for the old silk in them and the brocaded borders."

I began to roll up the painting. "Who is he?" I asked. "Do you know?"

Aimee glanced at the face. "I don't know," she said. "All I know is, his name is Yu. Everyone here is named Yu. They're all related to each other, and I'm related to all of them."

I closed the chest and locked it. The day was growing late, and I was glad when Aimee completed her inspection and her incense-burning, and we could lock up the temple and leave. The truth was I was beginning to feel increasingly ill at ease among my ancestors-in-law, all of whom seemed to be peering out at me from their tablet cases, in the gathering shadows.

That night, Aimee reported to the family on the condition of the temple. Major family conferences always took place at night, because that was the only time the whole family could be together. Besides, Aimee said, people were able to think better at night. The family decided that despite the cost, the temple must be repaired, as a last token of respect to the ancestors.

I didn't go back to it for several weeks. Although I knew that its roof had been mended, its windows restored, and its terrace weeded, I was taken by surprise when Aimee told me, one day, that the family had arranged for a special Buddhist ceremony, called the Feast of the Dead, to be held there the following night in her father's name. This ceremony is not primarily intended for the welfare of comfortable, well-cared-for souls, such as we trusted old Mr. Yu's to be, but is really an act of charity done on behalf of the person in whose name the ceremony is held, in order to increase his merits in the other world. It is a kind of mass for the ghosts of all the forgotten people who have died leaving no one among the living to worship them and weep for them, to feed them and look after the needs they have in that vast, shadowy place, where, it is believed, the dead, like babies, are helpless—always demanding and always hungry. This particular ceremony was also to be a sort of farewell to the ancestors, and, indeed, to the temple itself, because, Aimee explained to me, it was highly unlikely that the family would ever again be able to raise enough money to keep it in repair or hold ceremonies there for the dead.

On the night of the Feast, Aimee and I delayed somewhat in setting out for the temple—there was, as a matter of fact, no requirement that the whole family be present for all of the long ceremony, and we were among those members who chose to see only a portion of it—and the ritual was well under way when we arrived. The moon was three-quarters full in a sky as cold and clear as the water of the lake. The broken terrace, now weeded and cleaned, shone almost as white as the moon, except for a square of yellow light falling on it from the open doors of the temple. Within, we heard the sound of music and chanting.

The interior of the temple had changed considerably since I had last seen it. A long table covered with red silk stretched from the doorway to the altar. On it, at about the midway point, stood an elaborate wood-and-paper arch. Seated at the table, along both sides, were twenty Buddhist monks with shaven heads. They were dressed in red-and-black silk robes, and were chanting and playing musical instruments—gongs, bells, and drums. At the end of the table near us sat the head priest, his back to the door, wearing a golden crown from which hung long streamers of red-and-gold brocade.

The table was ablaze with the light of innumerable candles, whose smell of burning mutton fat combined with clouds of incense smoke to produce a stale and solemn odor. The members of the family were seated at random throughout the temple, on chairs that had been brought in for the ceremony. A few were trying to follow the chanting, either reading from texts of their own or looking over the shoulders of the monks at texts that were lying open on the table. The rest appeared bored. Ninth Sister was eating dried watermelon seeds, which she furiously cracked open between her teeth, while Third Sister knitted, almost as furiously. Second Brother and Second Sister's husband were involved in a dispute that, I could clearly hear over the chanting, concerned a missing chicken.

The tablets—the dead members of the family—were, as before, crowded on the altar, but now a few more of them stood upright, and those on the lower tiers had been lightly dusted. I immediately saw the two tablets that had just been added; they had been placed exactly in the middle of the lowest shelf, and were much cleaner than any of the older ones. Offerings of food and wine, no doubt intended for all the other ancestors as well, had been placed on the table in front of them. Moving closer to the tablets, I had my usual sensation of being as much looked at as looking. I had never inspected closely any of the latticed windows through which the ancestors presumably continued to view this world, and as I now went up and did so, I was sure I felt a light wind emanating from the whole altar, as if I were standing before the entrance to some subterranean cavern, and I moved away, back to where the candles made a brighter light.

Aimee had borrowed a copy of the ritual and now beckoned me. She was standing behind the head priest, who had before him on the table a large array of objects: a bronze zodiacal disk, tiny saucers of rice and oil, brass hand bells, a drum, blocks of wood carved into stylized fish shapes, a double-ended bronze mace, a bowl of water, several pieces of coarse millet bread, and an open text. At certain points in the chanted ritual, he would toss a grain or two of rice through the arch at the center of the table—the "spirit gate," through which the dead were to be summoned.

The ceremony was nearing its climax, Aimee told me, and now the monk began the summoning of the dead. I was quite satisfied that the dead were already there, but I listened respectfully as Aimee translated the classical text into simpler Chinese. The ghosts of the drowned, the frozen, the starved were called—the ghosts of lovers, suicides, children, and fishermen. Concubines and murdered emperors, beggars and widows were conjured up. The chanting stopped, then began again, at first slowly and then faster and faster. The room rang with the rhythmic alternation of drums and gongs. This was the final invocation before the offering of food to the great ghostly host gathered around us.

The hands of the head priest were not still for an instant. He would touch the surface of the oil with a fingertip, draw an invisible line across the bronze zodiacal disk, place three grains of rice on it, move them from one zodiacal sign to another, ring a bell, and toss the grains through the arch. Then, as swiftly, he would intertwine his fingers, folding and unfolding them, in a series of graceful gestures symbolic of towers of paradise, opening flowers, flames, and jewels. Suddenly, he picked up a bell and stood, ringing it. The chanting and the music stopped. Only the loud ringing of the bell continued for some twenty seconds, and then that, too, stopped. This was the point the ceremony had been moving toward, and it seemed entirely natural now that the priest should pick up the pieces of bread before him and toss them, with an underhand motion, one by one, through the arch.

The ghosts had been fed, and the ceremony was over. The priest sat down and lifted off his crown. The whole company began to move about and talk at once. The monks removed their robes, folding them carefully, and began to pack up their gongs and bells and prayer books. Most of the candles were put out. The monks left, followed by the family, except for Elder Brother, who lingered to light a few last sticks of incense before locking up. Outside, Aimee and I stood for a moment on the edge of the terrace looking at the moonlit lake, and then went back into the temple just as Elder Brother put out the last of the candles. In the darkness, the moonlight fell in swastika patterns across the floor and on the altar, where—I knew, rather than saw—a thousand private patterns of moonlight shone inside the black windows of the spirit tablets.

Elder Brother, Aimee, and I left the temple together, locking the gate behind us, and as it was late at night and we were in a remote part of the city, we had to walk a long way before we found pedicabs. Elder Brother took the lead cab, and Aimee and I followed. Our drivers, all strong young men, perhaps happy to have fares and to be traveling together through the empty moonlit streets, began to call out to one another: "Old turtle, move a little faster!" "Get out of my way!" "Lend your father room!" Challenged and encouraged, they raced together down the wide street. Our pedicabs swayed violently, the little oil lamps that served as warning lights bobbing under them. I had the distinct impression that I had just come from a party where everyone was very drunk. I felt drunk myself, and pleasantly relaxed and sleepy in the swaying cab. It seemed a fitting farewell to the ancestors, themselves left drunk on incense and wine, leaning against one another in their moonlit temple.

One summer afternoon, a month or so after the Feast at the temple, some friends invited me to go swimming with them in the New People's Swimming Pool. I had heard of this pool, although I did not know where it was, and knew that it had been open for one or two weeks. Carrying towels and bathing suits, my friends and I took pedicabs and turned north on the main street. Aimee was not along, and I had not heard the directions my friends gave, so I had no idea where we were going.

At the point where the main street turned west, our pedicabs continued northward and entered a dusty alleyway that seemed familiar to me. We crossed a stone bridge, and then I realized that we were following the route Aimee and I had taken to the Yu ancestral temple. I could already see the top of the north city wall. In a few moments, we emerged on the south shore of the lake, and I saw the Yu temple rising on its far side. The expanse of water between us and the temple was filled with rowboats and the splashings of several hundred bright-skinned bodies. The lake was a small one, and had been completely encircled, since I had last seen it, by a border of concrete following the line of the original shore in smooth, neat curves and undulations.

Where the terrace of the temple jutted out into the lake, the concrete had been laid to form steps up from the water, affording bathers access to the terrace, on which a number of people were now resting and sunbathing. A girl in a black bathing suit was poised on the end of a diving board set in a concrete platform next to the terrace. Our pedicabs had stopped at a couple of mat sheds, serving as bathhouses, on the shore directly opposite the temple, and from there I could see the gate in the temple's back wall that Aimee, Elder Brother, and I had gone through and locked with such finality on that last night. It was closed, and the temple itself appeared to be as silent and inscrutable as ever. I knew that the land had not been confiscated, and I could see that nothing had actually been built on the terrace itself, yet it was obviously meant to be used as part of the "pool's" facilities. Though the property seemed unmolested, I felt suddenly sure that it was not as we had left it, and I was surprised to discover that I was worried about the ancestors themselves, as if they were, after all, something real.

While my friends changed into bathing suits, I hired a boat at the water's edge. Without the gate key, there was no way of getting to the temple except by boat, but I felt that I must have a closer look. Leaving my friends behind, I rowed across the lake. As I came near the steps, I saw one of the double doors of the temple swing open and a couple of brown young men in scanty bathing trunks saunter out. For just a moment, I glimpsed the inside. I had an impression of a place more desolate and wrecked than it had been when I first saw it. It must have been curiosity or simple vandalism that had led the swimmers to break into it in the first place. Being closed on the land side by the locked gate, it was of no use to them as a bathhouse. I could not really tell the condition of the altar, but it seemed to me that only about half the ancestral tablets were on it. Wanting to learn no more, turning back just as I reached one end of the steps, I saw half a dozen of them bobbing in the water. I can only surmise that they were tossed there by swimmers amusing themselves, or perhaps even playing some sort of water game they had invented to pass the time.

That night, the moon, part full and straight above the rooftops, kept me awake. I slept, at last, to dream of the ancestors. Dressed in court robes and crowns and arrayed in shadowy tiers around me, they were angry and unhappy. Why had I not helped them, they asked? I had no answer and awoke, remembering the tinkle of antique crowns, the dry slither of silk, and the sadness, in a room filled, I saw, with my own private patterns of moonlight cast through the latticed windows.

LILY

THE PEKING Communist government undertook, amid a
storm of publicity, the reform of the city's prostitutes, described in the newspapers and over the radio as "unworthy of
a civilized nation," "feudal relics of capitalism," and "a blot
on the newly awakened Chinese people." The Chinese people
themselves were depicted, just then, as at their busiest, daily
rising up and advancing and wiping out, to the right and left,
social injustices of every kind. Unlike other "blots on the
Chinese people," often wiped out very thoroughly indeed, the
prostitutes, considered the innocent victims of a corrupted
society, were to be re-educated and placed back in the ranks
of productive labor.

In any country, I suppose, the restoration of fallen women
is something the average good citizen is likely to view with
emotion, but in the grimly puritanical climate of Communist
China, the government's anti-prostitution program, inaugu-
rated in student and worker discussion groups and brought
to full bloom in gigantic youth demonstrations where the
iniquities of the prostitution system were sensationally exposed to horror-stricken, even weeping boys and girls, a re-
forming spirit was created resembling, more often than not,
mass hysteria.

In the meantime, apparently unconcerned with these emotional excesses, the authorities bided their time, taking no ac-
tual steps until the public was sufficiently aroused. As usual,
the government hoped to create the illusion that its every

105

movement was made only after carefully consulting the wishes of the man in the street; and when the brothels were finally closed, it truly seemed to be an action that the great and virtuous Chinese people, the ultimate reservoir of the nation's wisdom and strength, had spontaneously demanded.

My wife's conservative family took an uncharacteristic interest in all this, not because they much cared what happened to the prostitutes, but because my wife's elder sister, a spinster of about fifty, was employed in the criminal section of the Ministry of Justice which had been made responsible for the custody of the girls until such time as the government decided how and where to go about rehabilitating them.

In the old days, before the Communists came to power, Elder Sister had worked in the ministry more to pass time than anything else. Through the influence of her powerful family, she had acquired an easy job to which she repaired in the morning around ten or eleven o'clock and left in the afternoon at three or four, depending on the weather and how she felt.

In those days, the wheels of justice turned exceedingly slow. A criminal case, which might easily have waited more than a year for the decision of a judge, could wait still another six months, until Elder Sister found the time to record the case and decision in her books and file the results in the proper pigeonhole over the desk. Only then could the accused, who had already spent a year or more in jail, be legally sentenced.

Elder Sister had a special pigeonhole for the death sentence and had created a certain notoriety for herself in the case of a man who, although sentenced to only three years in prison, narrowly escaped being shot on the Peking execution grounds because she had filed his case (it had been a rainy day) in the wrong hole. Although the old pigeonhole system of justice had been abolished, Elder Sister continued to work at the Ministry of Justice, not only because her family needed the money, but because the new authorities were obviously desperate for people with any training at all and would not allow her to quit.

Still, none of us could have imagined that the ministry could be so desperate for personnel as to choose Elder Sister to serve as a housemother in one of Peking's defunct brothels and, on the evening when she came home to pack a few belongings, with the news that she would be gone several weeks, the family was first astonished and then indignant.

While Elder Sister packed, her eight sisters and two brothers, as well as aunts, uncles, and in-laws, gathered together in the mansion's main reception hall to decide what to do. Aimee had brought me along. The great room, generally unused during the winter, was very cold. Wearing coats and padded gowns, Elder Brother, Aimee, and several of her sisters sat huddled around a large, icy-looking marble-topped table under the weak illumination of two light bulbs hanging high overhead in a pair of ornate glass and wood lanterns. The rest of us sat on chairs against the wall.

Everyone seemed to be talking at once. "They can't do this to her," someone was saying in a shrill voice. "It's unthinkable! Elder Sister was raised by old-fashioned standards. She knows nothing of these modern ideas." I had already heard a good deal from my wife about how strictly Elder Sister had been brought up, in part because she had been the first daughter, but chiefly because, during her girlhood when a Manchu emperor still occupied the throne of China, young ladies of breeding were required, by a rigid Confucian morality, to remain secluded in the inner chambers of their homes practicing a vast heritage of female crafts and virtues, the most important of which were, perhaps, fine stitching and submissiveness.

"She's more like Mama than any of the rest of us," one of the sisters went on. "Everyone said she was such a beautiful girl. She was as graceful as a Goddess of Mercy. Even Papa never found a man worthy to be her husband."

"That's why I worry about her," someone else said. "If she had married and understood these things I wouldn't mind so much, but she's a virgin."

"And *completely* innocent!" someone else said. Although I saw nothing in Elder Sister's appearance to indicate that she had ever been a goddess or even a beauty, she did look very virginal indeed. The long blue cotton gowns she wore hung within a few inches of her ankles and her hair, parted in the middle, was always tightly drawn into a bun at the back of her neck in the manner of old-fashioned Chinese women. Except for talcum powder, she wore no make-up and, although her ears were pierced, I never saw her wearing earrings. Instead, her only and invariable decoration was a jade-tipped pin that she kept tucked into her bun of slickly oiled hair. Such a pin, it had been pointed out to me, was sharper and longer than one might expect, and could function in an emergency as an effective weapon of defense. And yet, despite appearances, I wondered if her innocence of worldly affairs was as complete as the family assumed, and if they were not underestimating her knowledge, accumulated however haphazardly through the years, of matters never openly discussed.

Her sisters made their decision. She must quit her job at all costs.

Only Elder Brother disagreed. He could not allow her even to try to resign, he said. It was too dangerous. This government, he reminded his sisters, did not allow workers to quit or even to change jobs without an acceptable reason. If Elder Sister insisted on resigning, she would undoubtedly be investigated by the police and might even be drafted into one of those new white-collar labor battalions that were being sent to China's hinterlands daily. There was no question about it—she would be far better off in a nearby brothel. He admonished his sisters to face the facts realistically and not indulge in useless emotionalism. Naturally, in the old days, he would never have considered allowing her to perform such a task, but it was obvious that his only proper duty under present circumstances was to help prepare her for what she would find in the South City.

The sisters, looking contrite, had reluctantly submitted to the logic of their brother's argument, when Elder Sister, carrying an overnight bag, appeared in the doorway. Everyone fell abruptly silent.

"I'm leaving," she announced.

"Wait!" one of the aunts said. "Sit down a moment. We want to talk to you." Elder Sister came in reluctantly and sat down in a chair at the end of the marble table. She took out a box of matches.

"Who has a cigarette?" she asked. Elder Brother gave her a Ruby Queen. After lighting it, somewhat amateurishly I thought, she drew an enormous quantity of smoke into her lungs and then exhaled it slowly into the air over the table. Cigarette smoking was Elder Sister's only modernism, but she had taken to it with a vengeance, smoking, I had heard her sisters complain, some forty cigarettes a day.

"You know," the aunt continued, "you must take precautions in the South City against disease." Apparently feeling this to be an overly mysterious remark, she added, by way of explanation, "All those women have diseases, you know."

Elder Sister looked uncomfortable and concentrated on the end of her cigarette. "What diseases?" she asked.

Elder Brother cleared his throat. "White mud and plum poison," he said. "Those two."

"Oh," Elder Sister said. "Those two."

"Don't drink or eat out of their cups and dishes," Elder Brother said. "And don't pick up anything they've touched."

"All right," Elder Sister said.

"Don't talk to them," the aunt said, "and if they speak to you, don't answer."

"And wear your nose mask when you're in the same room with them," someone else told her. Elder Sister, as did many

Chinese, often wore a gauze surgical mask on the streets, the theory being that it not only filtered out dust and germs but, in winter, warmed the nose as well.

"All right," Elder Sister said, "I'll wear it."

"And most important of all," one of the sisters said, "don't smoke any of their cigarettes—even if they offer you one out of a fresh pack."

"It doesn't matter," Elder Sister answered, "I can't smoke, anyway. The office asked me not to as a good example to the girls."

"You'll still want to smoke in secret," the aunt insisted, "so promise not to smoke *their* cigarettes."

"I promise," Elder Sister answered in a subdued tone, apparently bringing her catechism to an end since no one had anything further to say.

We accompanied her to the main gate where she strapped her bag to the handlebars of her bicycle before pedaling off. "I'll try to phone tomorrow," she called back.

"Good-bye," the family called. "And remember," someone shouted just before she passed out of earshot, "don't smoke their cigarettes."

During the following days, we all thought and talked about nothing but Elder Sister and the prostitutes and, as a matter of fact, I had a little more to think about, I suspected, than anyone else in the family because I had actually been to the brothel in which Elder Sister was housemother. I kept this fact to myself, at the time, although I was sorely tempted, in the face of so much family speculation as to just what she must be facing in the South City, to describe to them, as well as I could remember, The House of Flowering Willows.

I had seen it late one winter evening some two years before in the company of four foreigners, one of them Hetta Empson. The five of us had been to a performance of Peking

Opera in the South City and, from there, had gone to a noisy four-storied restaurant where, on the top floor, we drank yellow wine and ate crisp fatty slices of roasted duck rolled with black bean sauce, and leeks in pancakes as thin and pale as powdered skin. One member of our party, an Englishman named John Blofeld, who had lived many years in Peking, had been obliged to answer a great many questions about the city. Toward the end of the meal, someone asked if Peking had a red light district, and John answered that the present district was quite close by, having been settled there some fifty years ago when its old quarters in another part of the city were burned out during the Boxer Uprising. "Isn't it true," someone else asked, "that Chinese brothels are really no more than teahouses compared to what we have in the West? I mean," he went on, "the women are more like entertainers, aren't they?"

John laughed. "I think you'd better go and have a look for yourself," he said.

"Well, naturally," Hetta said, "you men would know more about this sort of thing than I, but I *do* think it's unfair that men have *all* the fun. I've never even seen a brothel."

"In that case," John answered, "I think we'd all better go and have a look. It's quite safe, you know."

And so it was that we all went off to have a look at brothels, but not before John, who was to act as guide, explained that the brothels were divided into first-, second-, and third-class houses, and that, in order to complete our education, he would take us to one of each.

We hired pedicabs and arrived some ten minutes later at a cross street in what looked to be an unfrequented section of the South City. After dismissing the pedicabs, our guide peered first up one dark street and then down another before striking off southward. All the gates in the walls along both sides of the street were shut and dark, but it seemed to me that for such a late hour more people were lurking in the shadowy doorways and walking on the street than might be normally expected. Our guide suddenly turned about. He thought it must be the wrong street, he said. Back at the intersection, we struck off westward on another street, which looked much like the one we had just left. After walking some way along this one, he stopped again. "I'm afraid I'll have to ask someone," he said. "Do you mind?" We all assured him that we didn't mind at all, and Hetta said she was having great fun.

Furtively approaching a figure in a darkened doorway, he asked in Chinese, "Excuse me, but can you direct me to one of the brothels of this area?" The man in the doorway spat and, waving his arms in a circle, said in a hoarse voice, "They're all brothels."

"Oh, is that so? Then could I trouble you to point out a third-class house?"

The man stepped to one side and pushed open the gate behind him. "They're all third-class on this side of the street," he said. Beyond the gate, we found ourselves in a long tunnel-like passageway dimly illuminated along either side by lights glinting through windows, which appeared to be curtained with odd bits of old bedspreads and discarded underwear. "Old Aunty," someone called, "guests have come!" A fat old woman dressed in a black cotton padded gown appeared around a corner at the end of the passage. "Come in. Please come in," she called, waddling up to us on bound feet, an increasingly rare sight.

"We are tea guests," John said, using a phrase that, he later told us, meant that we had come prepared to pay a modest charge for the privilege of drinking tea and, at the same time, looking over the girls. This was an age-old custom, we were told, presumably enabling the discriminating customer to choose something fairer, plumper, or younger than he might otherwise hope to get. We were shown into a room at the passageway's far end where it opened onto a tiled courtyard. This court was completely surrounded on all four sides by galleries of rooms to the height of three stories and looked, in fact, rather like the restaurant we had just left.

The room we were ushered into contained a table, chairs, a coal stove, a kettle of boiling water, a dressing bureau, and a bed. In the middle of the table, on a tin tray, sat a tea canister, a cheap porcelain teapot, and several cups. The madam opened the canister, tossed some tea leaves into the pot, and poured it full of boiling water. With an air of having done the same thing many times before, she then distributed the cups in front of us and sat down herself to wait for the tea to steep. In the meantime we all looked at the bed.

Like most Chinese beds, it was large, had a wooden bottom, and was spread with quilts. There were more quilts, looking none too clean, neatly rolled at the foot of the bed, and there were two small pillows at the head, filled, I could guess, as were most cheap pillows in China, with the husks of grain. Tucked under the ear, this versatile pillow will produce, at even the slightest movement, the sound of crackling flames, the splatter of rain on leaves, or the sinister crunch of a booted foot.

While we were drinking our tea, the girls began to arrive. They passed, one by one, pausing for only a moment before the open door of our room. As each new girl appeared, the madam called out a name, "Jade Excellence," "Precious Purity," "Delightful Jar," "Fragrant Hairpin," and so on.

Although the girls passed too quickly for us to gain much of an impression, except that they all wore heavy make-up and seemed to have had their foreheads stenciled with the same pair of soaring, winglike eyebrows, we complimented the madam on their beauty, paid, and left.

Finding the next brothel, a second-class one, was much easier, and in a very short time we were sipping tea again while a new string of beauties passed our door. They looked much the same as the other girls. In fact, the only detectable difference between this brothel and the last was that our room here had a cover on the table and some blue peacocks embroidered on the bed quilts. Having thanked the madam for her tea and remarked on the beauty of her girls, we moved on to a first-class brothel.

The room where tea was served in this establishment, although by no means a luxurious one, displayed a bed containing enormous mirrors set into its head and foot. "Oh, look! It's just like a barber shop," exclaimed Hetta, leaning over to inspect her reflection, both fore and aft, in the mirrors.

"For God's sake," said John, "come and sit down!"

Apart from the mirrors, the *pièce de résistance* of this house was an English-speaking girl who, after being introduced to us, sat down and proceeded to display her linguistic proficiency by confessing, all in English, that she had had a G.I. boy friend, that he used to write her letters, but not any more, and that her name was Lily. "I very like American," she finished, leering at John. Lily was by no means a beautiful girl. Her mouth was too big and her eyes too small, and every inch of her thick and shining shoulder-length hair had been crimped into symmetrical zigzag waves as barbarically splendid as Nebuchadnezzar's beard and, as if that were not enough, spit curls framed her face. She was, in short, grotesque and yet mysteriously, even compellingly, attractive.

"Are you happy here?" Hetta asked her.

"Sure," Lily giggled behind her hand. "This good place. Everybody all-time happy here."

"What is the name of this place?" someone asked.

"You know, tree grow 'long side water," she said, "springtime, very pretty, this house name."

We tried, for a while longer to make sense out of Lily's unique syntax and then, complimenting the madam on the beauty of her girls and praising Lily for her fine command of our language, we tipped her, paid for the tea, and bade farewell to the last of our brothels.

As we were leaving, someone asked John, "What did she say the name of this place was?"

"The House of Flowering Willows," he answered.

At the time Elder Sister went off to the South City, I wondered if she would find Lily still there. But when Elder Sister came home for a short visit one afternoon a week later, I could think of no way of questioning her without disclosing my own adventure. All the family crowded round to hear what she had to say.

"First, give me a cigarette," she said. "I haven't smoked since I left." After the first couple of puffs, she grew dizzy, but quickly recovered. "It's terrible!" she exclaimed. "The girls hate me. *They're* the ones who won't speak to *me*, and I'm sure they wouldn't give me a cigarette even if I asked for one. Anyway, they weren't diseased at all," she said, "because they were already cured of anything they had by a traveling platoon of doctors and nurses before I got there. As far as I can see, they are healthier than most people."

Her first task, Elder Sister told us, had been to persuade the girls to change out of their skimpy, bright-hued silks and brocades into the sensible blue cotton padded uniforms issued to them by the government. At the first suggestion of such a thing, the girls had burst into tears. "We'd rather die now in our own clothes!" they had cried. When Elder Sister, passing over this, came to her second suggestion, which was that the girls allow their hair to be bobbed, they yelled, kicked, and swore. "They're going to shave our heads!" wailed one. "They want to disfigure us!" cried another. "Kill us now and be done with it, you rotten turtle's egg!" they screamed at Elder Sister. "Let us at least die all in one piece!"

Elder Sister sighed wearily, "And so they're still wearing their old clothes," she said, "and their hair is still uncut." She looked at her watch. "It's time to go back, and I don't know *what* I'm going to do."

Completely at a loss as to what advice to offer in a

situation where the virtues epitomized by Elder sister meant nothing, the family sadly saw her to the gate. "Anyway," someone said as Elder Sister pedaled away, "she should be proud that those girls don't like her. It shows she's a real lady."

During the following week, Aimee and I had occasion to go shopping in the central part of the city. It was after dark when we were ready to return home, and we tried to hire pedicabs at the intersection of the Avenue of Long Peace and what foreigners used to call Morrison Street, a locality favored by the presence of foreign-style restaurants, hotels, and theaters. Aimee called out our destination to the pedicab men gathered near the corner. "The West Four Archway, Crooked Hair Family Lane."

"Four thousand," one of the pedicab men called back, naming a fantastically high price. The other pedicab men who were pulled up beside him looked surprised. "I know where she wants to go," he said to them, "I've been there before."

Aimee and I, ignoring him, walked on to an open place where other pedicabs were coming forward to meet us, but we were intercepted by the same fellow, who pedaled up from behind and stopped in our path. "You'd better take me if you don't want trouble. After all, we're both Chinese," he said to Aimee, apparently assuming that I understood no Chinese, "and if you're making foreigner's money, why shouldn't I make a little too? What does it hurt you?"

Aimee stopped in astonishment. "What are you saying?" she asked in a loud voice. "What are you talking about?"

"You're no better than I am," the pedicab man answered in a nastier tone. "I know what you are."

Aimee was in a rage. "What are you saying to me, you dead dog!" she shouted. "Are you threatening me?" At that moment, another pedicab man, who had come up from the rear, interrupted, calling out, "She's one of the Yu family daughters. I know her. Leave her alone!" After we got home that night, the family discussed the incident at length without, however, arriving at any satisfactory explanation.

In the following week, Elder Sister came home for her second visit. She was in a triumphant mood. One of the girls had, at last, offered her a cigarette, which she had accepted, Elder Sister told us defiantly, bringing, by this one act, all her troubles to an unexpected end.

"It's not that they are so unlike you and me," she said. "It's only that they are really much more stupid than ordinary people and must be treated like children."

"I've heard that some of those girls can speak foreign languages," I said in as offhand a manner as possible. "Surely they aren't all so stupid?"

"Foreign languages!" Elder Sister exclaimed. "Where do you think I'm staying? In a university?"

"No, seriously," I said, "don't some of the girls speak English?"

"It's strange you should ask that," she said, "because there *is* one girl who insists that she speaks perfect English, but, of course, as I've never studied English, myself, I can hardly judge. She calls herself *Li-li* and says it's an English name. Does it mean something?"

"It's a girl's name," I told her. "Is she stupid, too?"

"She *is* smarter than the rest, it's true," Elder Sister said. "In fact, she's really a very good girl, and I'm particularly grateful to her, because she's the one who offered me the cigarette."

The cigarette had apparently been offered as a joke, but when Elder Sister accepted it and not only smoked it, but smoked it like a veteran, inhaling each and every puff deep into her lungs, the girls had been dumbfounded. From that moment, Elder Sister's success was assured. In the past, the girls had always balked at her orders, phrased as requests or suggestions, but when Elder Sister stopped making suggestions and, instead, gave direct orders, with a burning cigarette dangling from her lips, the girls literally leaped to obey.

"It has shown me," Elder Sister declared to us, "that, in all my life, the only really useful thing I have learned to do is smoke."

"How can you say that?" one of her sisters objected. "You've always been a model to the rest of us. We love you because you know so little about the world."

"Then you'd better find some other reason for loving me," Elder Sister replied, "because, in these weeks, I've heard a good deal. I've learned words you've never heard and I've learned what they mean, and what's more, I'm glad I've learned."

I was surprised to find Elder Sister's remark not hailed by a general outburst of indignation. On the contrary, the Yu daughters seemed inclined to admit that their sister had got one up on them, and when later I observed them going off alone with her to the Hall of Ancient Pines in the garden, I was not above suspecting that it was for the purpose of testing their worldly knowledge against Elder Sister's new vocabulary.

One evening, a few days after Elder Sister returned again to her brothel, Aimee and I were involved in a second pedicab incident. We had been to a movie and returned home late, hiring pedicabs at a modest price outside the entrance to the Easter Peace Market.

The pedicab men seemed rather gay about the haul. If they had been very young, I might not have been suspicious, but they were up in years, and I could see nothing for two grown men to be so pleased about at the prices we were paying.

"We've got something, haven't we?" one called out, and the other answered, "We've certainly got something extra."

"That's right," answered the first one.

They passed a great many more remarks of this nature, until finally one of them said, "Anyone who wants to keep a secret, naturally has to pay a little more. Isn't that right?"

"That's right," answered the other just as we stepped out at our gate. Aimee, too, I saw, realized something was up, and she tried to pay them the price we had fixed, but they wouldn't accept it.

"Come, come, little sister," the first man said. "We've pulled you a long way. You can't get away with paying us this little bit. We want five thousand." They were not asking for a tip, but for over twenty times the amount we had bargained for. The gate was barred from the inside, and I called to the gateman to open up, but he was apparently sleeping too well to hear.

"You do what we ask," one of the men said to Aimee, "or we'll break your bones."

"Open the gate!" I shouted, pounding on the huge red lacquered panels.

"I'll grind you to mincemeat," the other said, starting to get off his seat.

"Police! Police!" Aimee called in a voice even louder than mine. The police did, from time to time, pass on patrol along our street but, until now, I had always looked on them as a source of trouble rather than protection.

"Police! Police!" I shouted along with Aimee. "Open the gate. Help!" We both made so much noise that the pedicab man who was getting off his seat stopped in astonishment. I don't think either of them had expected us to create such a furor, and had only been trying to bluff us.

We were at our noisiest when the gateman, still half-asleep and fastening his pants, opened the gate, and Aimee and I retired behind its high threshold. She told him to go and find the police at once, whereupon, he ran stumbling down the street clutching at his pants, calling, "Police, police, police!"

The pedicab men looked even more surprised at this, but as we were about to outbluff them at their own game, they had "face" to consider and stuck their ground, yelling insults at us, or Aimee, rather. Curiously, they had very little to say about me, except that I was a foreigner, which Aimee and I knew very well, and that I had a great deal of money, which was certainly news to both of us.

In a very short time, a party of police (they always patrolled in groups) arrived, led by our gateman. "There!" he said. "Those two."

Aimee stepped out. "We hired these pedicab men at the Eastern Peace Market for two hundred apiece and now they demand five thousand," she said.

"Five thousand!" one of the policemen said. "That can't be true!" He turned to the pedicab men. "How much did you ask for just now?"

"Five thousand," one of them answered sulkily. "That's not too much for a foreigner. He must be paying her a lot more."

"Paying me!" Aimee shouted. "I'm his wife!"

"Never mind," the policeman said to Aimee. "I'll take care of this. You two fellows come along with us," he told the pedicab men. Not until they were gone and we had closed our gates, did we realize that the pedicab men had ended up with no payment at all.

During the following week, Elder Sister left the brothel and returned home for good. She was ecstatic. The girls, in uniform and with their hair bobbed, had at last been taken away to a factory dormitory and were, at that very moment, she told us, working in what the government called "productive labor" in a People's Button Factory.

"Did Lily go, too?" I asked.

"Yes. *Li-li*, too," she said. "But she will get into trouble, I think. She is stubborn and keeps her own opinions. She says she doesn't want to make buttons, and refuses to attend the political indoctrination classes with the other girls. I hope nothing bad happens to her."

We were all pleased to have Elder Sister home again, and when the prostitutes' play was produced a month later, the entire family conducted her, as the guest of honor, to see it. This was a play about the life of prostitutes in which all the roles were taken by the reformed prostitutes themselves, and we were hoping to see some of Elder Sister's girls in it.

The audience, as usual in any of Peking's theaters not devoted to the classical drama, was composed almost entirely of student and labor groups, which had had seats assigned to them in blocks. In the place of an afternoon or evening spent discussing Marxian dialectics or the true meaning of Sino-Soviet Friendship, these conversation-study groups were often sent to the new drama theaters where the actors continued to talk on-stage about much the same sort of thing. I had also heard that audiences in these theaters sometimes indulged in emotional displays, similar to the floor-rolling conversions of old-time revival meetings. It seemed unlikely, though, that the ex-prostitutes would have what it took to inspire such spiritual ecstasies.

The curtain opened revealing a set borrowed from one of the many Chinese productions of Gorky's *Lower Depths*. It was the interior of a brothel, where we found the girls in a large dormitorylike room huddled together to keep warm, because they were given nothing but the scantiest of rags to wear, except when a wicked madam called them out to minister to some depraved offstage customer.

The major portion of the play was concerned with how very, very badly the girls were treated by the old hag who was a personification, it was made clear to us, of *some* of the evils of the old capitalistic society. Toward the end of the play, the suffering of all exploited people was symbolically

121

concentrated in one of the girls. This girl, dying of tuberculosis, was so ill she couldn't leave her ragged bed, and was such an obvious financial loss that, rather than continue to feed her, the old hag popped her, still alive, into a jerry-built coffin and nailed down the lid, while the rest of the girls stood against the splotched, cheesecloth walls, shaking their shoulders and making sobbing sounds into handkerchiefs clutched to their faces.

Although the dying girl had been packed away out of sight, she was still very much with us, because we could hear her groaning inside the coffin. Her groans grew weaker, until they could barely be heard beneath the sobbing of the girls, when suddenly the murky, underworld air was rent, from offstage, by an unsteady rooty-toot-toot, presumably meant to be the clarion call of an army bugle. It was the People's Liberation Army, of course, arrived in the nick of time. The hag cowered, knocking against the scenery. And, in a very short time, what with more bugles and some soldiers (actually, more prostitutes in soldier's uniforms) everyone (except the old hag, who got dragged off) was beside herself with happiness, enlightened by a transcendental understanding of Marxian creed, miraculously cured of a host of diseases, and off to the button factory.

Elder Sister kept telling us that it hadn't happened that way, at all. The only thing she recognized, she said, was one of her girls on the stage, a girl who was not Lily, I was disappointed to see.

The acting of the girls was sadly unconvincing, except for the astonishment on the face of the old hag when she leaped aside to avoid a rock that had been hurled at her from out of the audience. For what purpose a rock came to be brought into the theater in the first place, I couldn't guess, but it clattered noisily across stage, causing the dying girl to forget her next lines, while the hag glared indignantly at the audience.

I had previously heard that the villains in the new drama theaters were often physically assaulted by audiences so infuriated that they had, in one instance, clambered over the footlights and seriously injured an actor.

But even the rock was not enough to distract me from the real performance taking place in the middle rows of the theater across the aisle to our right, which were occupied by some thirty or forty serious-looking young students, all members apparently, since they had come together, of the same discussion group.

At the time they first trooped into the theater, I had felt in them that extra intensity of dedication, a poised-on-the-brink, arid, unlovely soulfulness distinguishing those initiated to the giddy spiritual heights of socialistic perfection. The symbols of this new elite, the compressed lips, the knitted brow, the searching look in the eyes, were becoming more and more the vogue in Peking and, fortunately for the ambitious, could be easily imitated.

The boys in the aisle across from me were not pretending, I was sure. They breathed a thinner, rarer air than the rest of us, it seemed to me, and as the play progressed they proved me right.

While the hag went through her paces on the stage, cursing and beating the girls, the boys across from me seemed to be reacting not so much to the play as struggling with their own inner demons. Tears streamed from their eyes, and their faces were contorted in agonies of fury and uncontrollable despair. They writhed in their seats, cried out unintelligible guttural sounds, and gasped for breath. I had not expected so much genuine emotion, and turned completely around in my seat to watch them. One of the boys on the row nearest to me began to tremble violently, as if a current of electricity were passing through his body, and his eyes rolled back, leaving only the whites staring at the stage. Suddenly, as if the voltage had been turned full on, he arched out of his seat and toppled over into the aisle, where he lay absolutely rigid, although apparently still alive, since his heels clattered on the floor and foam bubbled from the corner of his mouth.

This created a certain commotion, but ushers quickly rushed down the aisle and carried him out as easily as if he had been a plank of wood. His groaning, twisting companions, immersed, it seemed, in the interior ecstasies of their own souls, had paid no attention at all. They were beyond noticing anything, I soon discovered, because in a few minutes, fits and convulsions spread through the whole group. To my amazement, no sooner did one keel over in his seat, foaming at the mouth, to be carried away, than another followed suit. Some three or four of them had passed into convulsions and had been carried out, when an older man, sitting in the first row of the balcony, got up and addressed the audience. "Comrades!" he called out, "restrain yourselves! This is only a play!" The play practically stopped. The sobbing girls dropped their handkerchiefs and frankly stared, open-mouthed, into the audience. Only the offstage bugler, on cue, and unaware evidently of all that was going on out front, rescued the performance and the audience, from helpless chaos.

"Really," Elder Sister said as we left the theater, "it didn't happen that way at all. Why have they changed everything? Everyone knows the brothels were closed this year. How can they show the Communist army liberating them the year before last?" No one answered.

We all took pedicabs. Ninth Sister had hired her pedicab separately a little ahead of the rest of us and, although we could see it in the distance, her pedicab was traveling much faster than ours and, after a while, passed out of sight. When we arrived home, however, Ninth Sister, excited and flushed, was waiting at the gate. "I know now, Fourth Sister," she said to Aimee, "why those pedicab men demanded more money the other night." We walked into the house together, while Ninth Sister breathlessly told her story. The pedicab man she

had hired at the theater had thought she was alone and, just
before he got to Crooked Hair Family Lane, had said, "You
see, I'm a fast pedaller. I go everywhere. If you promise me a
commission, I can bring you first-class customers."

Ninth Sister had been too astounded to speak. Besides, she
told us, she was curious and decided to keep quiet. When the
pedicab man arrived at Crooked Hair Family Lane, instead of
asking where she lived, he passed the Yu family gate and continued on down the street.

"Can you guess? He took me straight to the door of one
of those rented houses opposite the Wang mansion!" Ninth
Sister exclaimed. "He was very surprised when I told him I
didn't live there, and he was even more surprised when I told
him to come back and stop in front of this gate. 'But this is
the mansion of old Justice Yu!' he said.

" 'Yes, of course it is,' I told him, 'and I'm his daughter,
and I want to know what you meant by those things you said
to me, and I want to know who lives in that other house you
took me to?'

" 'I can't tell such things to a young lady like you,' he said.

"Our gateman had come out, so I said, 'Then tell it to him.
He's not a young lady,' and I went inside to wait." She paused
for breath. "You should *hear* what he told our gateman!"

"What *did* he tell him?" Aimee asked.

"He said that the other house was a house of black gates!"
she told us, with the air of one who expects to produce a
sensation.

"A house of black gates?" I asked.

"And furthermore," Ninth Sister went on triumphantly,
"most of the pedicab men know there are black gates on this
street somewhere, even if they don't know exactly where. As
far as they're concerned it *could* be our house. After all, a lot
of women live here."

"What are black gates?" I asked again.

"A red gate today can be a black gate tomorrow," someone

125

said mysteriously. "One never knows." It was Aimee who finally explained to me that a "black gate" was the name given to any house, usually situated in a residential area, where an independent woman sets herself up in business as a prostitute.

"Do you mean they paint their gates black as a sign?" I asked.

"I think it's just a name," Aimee told me. "After all, even respectable people might paint their gates black and it wouldn't mean anything."

Ninth Sister was still going breathlessly on, "And there are black gates all over the city now. There always were a few, the pedicab man said, but since the closing of the brothels they have sprung up everywhere."

"Don't the police know about it?" someone asked.

"Perhaps they do and perhaps they don't," Ninth Sister answered. "He didn't know."

It struck me as unbelievable that the police, who had complete control over the comings and goings of even the most humble and inconspicuous of Peking's citizens, should know nothing about the black gates. It seemed more reasonable to suppose that the whole business of closing the brothels had been to remove any possible hint that the authorities tolerated prostitution, in even a semiofficial form. Afterward, whether prostitution continued underground or not, it was of no more concern to them, since they had already made their point and extracted every ounce of favorable propaganda. As a matter of fact, I could guess the local police probably welcomed the black gates as a providential source of squeeze, all too scarce in the New China. But an even better reason for the apparent unconcern of the police, it occurred to me, was that it would have been imprudent, if not foolhardy of them, to continue to suppress, at that time, a vice so recently and so loudly proclaimed by the government to be nonexistent.

Whatever the reason, the house of black gates was undeniably there, and it seemed to me to be the final insult to Elder Sister. She had performed an unpleasant duty sincerely and as best she knew how and, as thanks, had not only been publicly betrayed in the theater, but was now being required to play the fool in her own backyard by a government that had never had, it now appeared, any discernible motive beyond its own aggrandizement.

We had been proud of Elder Sister and pleased to see her so proud of herself. We could have wished, therefore, that Ninth Sister had been a little less joyful about being the harbinger of such disillusioning news and, when Elder Sister said good night and went off to bed, looking confused and unhappy, we felt embarrassed and out of sorts.

The truth was that we had all been made fools of, and, in the following days, we tried to put the whole episode of the prostitutes out of mind. I might have forgotten the whole thing had I not gone with Aimee the following spring to a pleasure garden called the North Sea Public Park to watch a fireworks display over what had, in the past, been one of Peking's three imperial lakes.

We found a bench situated at the end of a dark, unfrequented path on a remote part of the shore, and had been sitting there for some time, watching cascades of stars and fiery flowers exploding overhead when, during a lull in the performance, I decided to go and buy some ice cream at the main gate.

I bought two ice cream cups, being careful to get two wooden spoons to go with them, and had come halfway back along the darkest part of the path, when there was a rustling in the bushes slightly ahead of me and a girl stepped out. "*Wai!* Hey!" she called softly in Chinese. "Why are you hurrying so? Wait a while." There was a light a little way ahead on a pole beside the path and, hurrying along, I quickly came out under it. The girl, still beside me, grabbed my arm. "Wait," she said. I stopped in the comparative safety of the light and looked at her. Although she was dressed in pants and her hair was uncurled and short, she had the big lips and impish eyes I remembered in Lily.

Under the light she looked me up and down. Until then, she hadn't realized that I was not Chinese. "Jeezus" she said in English. "A Russian! I very no like Russian," and disappeared back into the bushes. Holding out my cups of melting ice cream, I hurried on down the dark path, while overhead a sudden burst of huge purple and white flowers filled the black sky.

DOGS, MAH-JONGG, AND AMERICANS

For a time, after I moved into the Yu family mansion, the local police seemed content to let me come and go as I pleased, even though I was an American. Then, in the spring of 1950, my life, as well as that of almost everyone else in Peking, came under stringent control. Restrictions were placed on travel, new taxes were imposed, and all Chinese citizens were required to register with the police. Foreigners living in Peking not only had to register but had to submit to a police interview, in which they were asked who their friends were, what books they read, what kind of radio they had, what kind of camera, what kind of weapon (if they had no gun, then did they, perhaps, have a sword?), and what they thought of Marxism.

The government harassed foreigners as a matter of policy, and seemed to enjoy it. I was certain, however, that I had done everything officially required of me by the new laws. I had registered with the Central Department of Public Safety, where I declared that I had no camera or weapon of any kind, that my radio was a six-tube long-wave General Electric that gave me a shock whenever I touched two control knobs at the same time, and that, not having read Marx, I was unqualified to give an opinion of Marxism. After I had turned in new photographs of myself, along with my passport and various official documents dating from the time before the Communists came to power, the police issued me a residence permit, on the understanding that I was to leave China, with my wife, as soon as her family affairs were settled. In the meantime, I was fortunate, I felt, to be living in her house.

Behind the high walls of the Yu mansion, I felt little apprehension, despite the fact that the United States had closed its consulate, and all American citizens still remaining in Peking had been made charges of the British. On the contrary, when I was inside the mansion's quiet, book-filled studies, or in the stately reception halls, or in the garden, where we sat through the hot summer afternoons on rattan chairs under the trees, sipping synthetic lemonade and beguiled by the screech of cicadas and the murmur of our own voices, what went on outside the walls had almost no effect on my sense of well-being. If anything, the days were too uneventful.

Luckily, old Aunt Chin was there. She slept badly, and could be found at almost any hour of the day or night sitting up with a cat or two in her lap, and puffing on an asthma cigarette while she played complicated variations of solitaire with herself or rummy with Auntie Hu. My wife and I often joined them in their suite of rooms and would play Russian poker or auction bridge with them far into the warm summer nights while the great house slept.

I enjoyed those evenings. Aunt Chin, her thick, straight-bobbed gray hair swept back and held behind her ears by two tortoiseshell combs, would keep up an amazing flow of chatter. It was a point of pride with her, as with many recluses, to know better than anyone else what was going on in the world. On one such night, she got off on the subject of mah-jongg.

"I'd like to know what business it is of *theirs*," she said, meaning the new government, "if I want to play mah-jongg. I've played mah-jongg all my life, and no one ever told me before that it was a crime." Plainly visible under a table in a corner of the room were two mah-jongg sets in blockwood boxes. A few weeks earlier, the Communists had banned the game throughout China as a waste of labor hours. Although Aunt Chin had stopped playing the game, she evidently saw no reason to hide the sets. Besides, none of us knew just what the penalty was for playing mah-jongg. And, for that matter, we weren't absolutely sure that the authorities didn't also disapprove of card playing.

"Imagine those black devils up there," Aunt Chin went on, rolling her eyes toward the ceiling, "sneaking over the rooftops and listening at the eaves." Aunt Chin might have been talking about the bogeymen in some fairy tale, but she was in fact talking about figures in real life, the Night People—black-clad ex-burglars and acrobats who, so we had all heard, were employed by the police to scale the walls of private houses and detect from the rooftops the giveaway clatter of mah-jongg tiles or the equally telltale odor of opium. (Opium smoking was, of course, also prohibited, unless addiction could be proved, in which case an opium ration was supposed to be issued. Not many people, though, had the courage to try to prove themselves addicts.) It was rumored, further, that the Night People, with the help of the police, had marked off the city in sections and, working over one section each night, could cover the whole of Peking in less than a month.

"Moonlit nights and dogs are the only things that stop them," Aunt Chin said. "I've never liked dogs," she added, "but I admit I feel safer these days knowing old Baldy is around somewhere."

Baldy was our house dog, who, as a result of old age, or possibly a disease, had lost much of his hair. Occasionally, I would hear him give a shaky bark or two in the middle of the night, but he slept most of the time. Still, Aunt Chin was convinced that Baldy was our greatest single protection against the Night People, and she may have been right, because it was true that the Communist authorities hated dogs to the extent of instituting a citywide anti-dog campaign. Dogs were unproductive, they said, and ate an unearned share of the food raised by that paragon of all virtues, the Chinese peasant. I think the Communists really hated dogs because in a very tangible way the dog, loyal to individuals and not to beliefs, represented the last defense of the private citizen against the increasing nosiness of the police, the community, and the state. As a result, the Communists, besides insisting on the licensing of dogs, investigated and taxed the owners. How, the owners were asked, could they afford to feed a dog? Had they no shame about feeding dogs while human beings starved? Where did they get the money to keep a dog? And so on. In the end, the owner usually found it easier (as the authorities had expected he would) to quietly get rid of his dog, while the dogs kept by stubborn owners would often mysteriously disappear or be found poisoned.

The dogs of Peking had thus grown scarce, and precious to those few who still had them, so it was not just a dog that Aunt Chin was talking about but the only protector, halt and old though he was, of our right to smoke opium and play mah-jongg, to beat our children and keep secrets, to stand on our heads in the morning if we wanted to, and sleep in green and purple pajamas at night. Although Aunt Chin claimed not to like dogs, she had begun to feed this one from her own hands, and Baldy had come to love her more than anyone else in the family, looking at her with sad moist eyes, in a way her cats never did. Then, one morning a few days after Aunt Chin's remarks about the Night People, old Baldy was nowhere to be found, and when, at the end of a week, he still had not been located, the family felt that it had lost something of great value, as indeed it had.

On an especially hot evening, a week or so after Baldy's disappearance, Aimee and I joined Aunt Chin and her companion in their sitting room and found a guest—old Mme. Wang, another zealous mah-jongg and card player, who lived near us down the street. I had met her before, and had been impressed by her thin plucked eyebrows arching in almost perfect semi-circles over a soft powdered face that sagged gently, like slowly melting wax. That night, her face, powdered even more than usual, was compressed in a look of intense concentration as she and Aunt Chin sat at the card table apparently playing dice. "Up-up," Mme. Wang was saying as we moved our chairs to the table. "Seven," called Aunt Chin as the dice rolled to a stop. "Down-up," said Mme. Wang, who, I now noticed, was reading from a small and worn blue book. "Ten," Aunt Chin called. "Middle-down," the other old lady answered, and flipped to the back of the book, saying to herself, "Up-up, down-up, middle-down. Ah, here it is. 'The hidden is disclosed,' it says. 'The known concealed.' "

"Read the counter-reference again," Aunt Chin said.

Mme. Wang turned a few pages and read, " 'Rise and walk; disturb the dew.' "

Aimee explained to me that they were telling a kind of fortune with the book and dice, which Mme. Wang had brought over. First a question would be asked. Then the dice would be rolled several times, and the numbers obtained would lead to two quotations from the book. The way the quotations fitted together was supposed to indicate the answer, in somewhat the same way, it seemed, that the intersecting of latitude and longitude gives location.

Aimee asked what the question had been, and Aunt Chin told us that they had asked where to find old Baldy.

"What is the answer?" I asked.

"I have to think about it," Aunt Chin said. "It takes time."

In a short while, Mme. Wang left, after carefully wrapping her book and dice in a square of faded blue silk, and we started a game of bridge. During our second rubber, Aunt Chin, whose partner was her companion, appeared to be thinking hard about the fortune; she actually fluffed a trick and lost a little slam. Looking cross, she leaned back and lit an asthma cigarette. It was her deal but no one mentioned it, and we had sat in silence for some time when she suddenly said, in a burst of weedy-smelling smoke, "The dog may be in the garden."

"Why?" I asked, relieved that she had spoken at last.

"The fortune says, 'Disturb the dew.' And the only dew around here is in the garden."

This sounded to me like an unnecessarily literal interpretation, but I didn't say so, and we continued the game. Aunt Chin and her companion rapidly improved their score, and Aimee and I were far behind when we stopped playing, around eleven o'clock. This was early for us, but it was too hot to sit still any longer, and Aimee and I decided, quite apart from what Aunt Chin had said, to take a stroll in the relative coolness of the garden before going to bed.

We followed a white pebble path, just visible in the faint starlight, to a terrace on the edge of one of the garden's two empty pools, where we sat for a while on a stone slab, still warm from the heat of the day, and watched the fireflies appear and disappear in the long, damp grass. East of the garden towered the huge, upcurling roofs of the outbuildings of the sprawling Yu home. I could clearly see the silhouettes of the ridgepoles, surmounted at either end by great decorative tiles in the shape of fish, their tails turned up against the starlit sky. Aimee and I had not spoken for some time, and I was idly looking at the shadow of the nearest fish when I saw, just as clearly, another shadow. I pressed Aimee's arm, and she, too, looked toward the rooftops. Surreptitiously the shadow of a man had joined that of the fish on the rooftop nearest us. Then we saw the man's shadow glide up and across the ridge and disappear down the far side. We waited, but he did not return.

Indisputably, we had seen one of the Night People, but when, a few minutes later, we told the family, they said there wasn't much that anyone could do about it. Aunt Chin said there was no doubt now that old Baldy was dead, because otherwise the Night People wouldn't have dared to come. I lay in bed that night listening into the silence—aware, for the first time, that in our own house and in all the houses surrounding us no dogs were barking and that above us, over the sleeping mansion, the heavy eaves, soaring like protective wings outward and upward into the night sky, concealed in their ponderous grace the deceit and betrayal that I felt would ultimately defeat us all.

It seemed much later in the night when Aimee woke me, saying, "Something is happening outside. Listen!" I sat up and listened for a few moments, hearing nothing. Then, abruptly, in the blackness of the courtyard outside our bedroom window I saw the swift movement of a light. Slipping out of bed, I made my way, without turning on a lamp, to our sitting room, where the only door to our suite, a partly glass one, opened onto a tiled terrace. I was standing with my face pressed against the glass, trying to see into the darkness outside, when I felt the knob gently turn.

Nothing happened. The door was locked, and I wondered what I should do next—or, rather, what the person outside was going to do next. It suddenly occurred to me that the terrace light was controlled by a switch just inside the door, and I snapped it on, almost as a reflex action, without considering whether or not it was the wise thing to do.

As in a flash photo of a nocturnal animal that has tripped the mechanism of a camera, some ten men were illuminated on the terrace in a weird tableau—frozen for a moment in a parody of stealth, embarrassed and confused by the light. The fact that half of them were carrying carbines made them appear—at that moment, anyway—no less foolish. Our gatekeeper was in the middle of them, looking very unhappy, and I could guess what had happened. Later on, Aimee and I were able to piece out the events of the entire night.

Members of the military police, together with the local police—all of whom represented the People's Soldiers of China—had made a surprise raid on our section of the city after it had first been reconnoitred by the Night People (who, no doubt, had themselves been preceded by the dog exterminators), and were systematically checking all residents, house by house. Admitted by our helpless gateman, the soldiers had, of course, not allowed him to give warning, and, wherever possible, had contrived to enter our bedrooms without waking us beforehand. Several of the members of our household had been roused out of a sound sleep by the cold touch of a carbine muzzle at the back of the neck, and Aunt Chin's companion actually succumbed to hysterics. After awakening the sleepers, the police had demanded to see their registration papers.

At the moment I surprised the soldiers by turning on the terrace light that night, they were obviously trying to get into the sitting room of our suite, and just as I was beginning to feel that perhaps I had not done the most tactful thing, Aimee switched on the overhead light behind me, destroying my advantage, and unfastened the door. One by one, the soldiers entered the room, looking as if they expected a grenade to be tossed at them. Aimee, who had already put on a dress, was busy turning on the floor lamps when I left the room to put something on over my pajamas.

Perhaps it was because a carbine-armed soldier followed me to the bedroom that I chose to wear an enormous blue-brocaded dressing gown Aimee had made for me from a robe that had been worn at the imperial court by one of her ancestors. It expressed my feelings toward the People's Soldiers at that moment. If I could have found the sable hat topped with peacock feathers that originally went with it, I might have put that on, too, but even without it my splendor was impossible to overlook, and when I re-entered the sitting room, the soldiers seemed startled and moved uneasily aside.

One of them, a grim-looking officer, asked for my papers—all of them, those written in English as well as those in Chinese—and I gave them to him. He appeared to read each of them very thoroughly, but, since he read them all at the same speed, it wasn't hard for me to guess that he didn't understand a word of English. Then he asked for my police registration. I pointed to my residence permit, which he held, and said that I had registered with the police in the Central Department of Public Safety in order to get it.

"But this is not a *police* registration," he said. "Do you mean that you have not registered with the local police?"

I explained that the Central Police Bureau had told me that that was unnecessary.

His face became grimmer. "As far as we can see," he said, "you have no proper papers explaining your presence in this house."

"But he is my husband," Aimee said, "and this is *my* house"—an observation that, of course, represented a hopelessly old-fashioned way of looking at the situation. No one even bothered to answer her.

"Can't you telephone the central police?" I asked. "They know I live here."

"The Central Police Bureau does not open until seven in the morning," he said.

Aimee, in a last effort to save the day, said, "My husband doesn't speak Chinese very well. I'll go with him the first thing in the morning to see that he registers with the local police."

Considering that we had all along been speaking Chinese and that I felt I had spoken rather well, I was a bit put out. Then my interrogator said, "He will have to come with us now," and I suddenly realized what Aimee had been trying to forestall.

Turning to her, I said very loudly in English, "What did he say?"

"He said . . ."

"I *know* what he said. What do I do now?" I continued, in English.

"Oh." She looked at the police officer. "Can't he wait until morning?" she asked.

"No. He must be taken into police custody until he can be properly checked."

She looked back at me and said, "I'll come with you. Don't worry." I thought she hadn't tried very hard, but, from experience, was confident that she knew when argument was useless, if not actually harmful.

Without giving me time to change from my brocaded robe, four of the soldiers formed a guard around me, two in front and two behind. In this formation, with Aimee behind us and the rest of the soldiers following her, we moved out through the front gate, while our gateman looked on as if I were being led to execution. The police station for which we were headed was only at the end of the street, and we were marching along briskly when Aimee called out to the soldiers around me, "It's not necessary to *run* to the police station." She had decided, I supposed, that since I was going to be taken to the station anyway, she could be as unpleasant as she liked. "Walk as fast as I do and no faster!" she ordered, and, moving to the head of the formation, she immediately slowed her pace. The soldiers, to my surprise, followed suit, whereupon Aimee, muttering under her breath like an irritable squad leader, led us the rest of the way at her own speed.

I was not the only catch that night. The police station was full of people in every state of dishabille. They were standing in the center of a large room, and all of them turned to look when I was brought in. I was the only foreigner present, and, of course, I was still wearing the luminous imperial robe. All the chairs and benches in the room were occupied by soldiers resting between forays into the sleeping neighborhood. Stopping in front of one of the soldiers, whose mouth at once dropped open, Aimee asked, in a loud voice, "Are there no chairs? Do you drag us out of our beds in the middle of the night and expect us to stand till morning?" The openmouthed soldier and the one beside him got hastily to their feet, and Aimee sat down, beckoning me to sit beside her.

As soon as I sat down, a red-faced boy in uniform sitting on the other side of me smiled shyly and offered me a cigarette. I took it gratefully, since I had brought none of my own. "What is your worthy nation?" he asked, using the polite honorific, which by then had been practically eliminated from Chinese speech as a feudalistic anachronism.

It was my turn to be shy. "My humble country is America," I told him.

He continued to smile. "China loves the American people. They are misled by their government but they are good people," he said. Even though I knew that this was the Party line at the time, I was impressed by the warmth of his smile, and I wondered if he had been drinking.

Aimee asked how I felt, and I told her I felt fine. "Don't you want anything?" she asked. "Wouldn't you like something to eat?" It hadn't occurred to me that I would be allowed to eat in a police station, and I said so, but Aimee replied that no one would mind, and, getting up, she started for home. Presently, she returned with some sandwiches. Later, she went back for cigarettes, and once again to bring me a murder mystery, and as the sky began to brighten, she returned a fourth time, with warm sugared milk and twisted strips of dough fried in sesame-seed oil. Nothing we said or did or ate went unnoticed, and I was aware that her solicitude for me did not please the officers in charge.

After a while, I became interested in the detective story Aimee had brought me, and by the time I had finished it, the sun was well up and a new group of police, yawning and stretching—the daytime force, I supposed—were coming down from what was obviously their sleeping quarters upstairs. Among them was a young girl, perhaps twenty years old, wearing a police uniform. Her face was smooth and pink, her hair bobbed. She swaggered like a man. I suspected that she was well aware of the rather unusual presence of a foreigner, because she pointedly avoided looking at me.

Walking over to a worried-looking old man, she addressed him in a chummy manner, and some of the worry left his face. "Where are you from, Granddad?" she asked, and, as all Chinese do, he answered by naming the place of his family's origin. "Shantung Province," he said.

"Where were you born?" she asked.

"Tientsin," he said.

"Is that your home now?"

"Yes."

She began to swing her arms. "Then what are you doing in Peking?" (Since the city had been made the capital of Communist China, its old name, Peking [Beijing], which means Northern Capital, had been restored, and the name Peiping, or Northern Peace, invented in 1926 when the Kuomintang government moved the capital to Nanking, had passed out of use on the Chinese mainland.)

"I'm staying with a friend," he answered.

"I asked what you're *doing* here?"

"Oh, I . . ." he said, wetting his lips with the tip of his tongue. "I'm trading a little."

"Trading in what?"

"Flour."

Her arms went on swinging as she continued to question him, and her face, though still smooth and pink, looked strangely older. I changed my estimate of her age. She might have been over forty.

In the course of the interrogation, she gradually accelerated the speed of her questions to a point where it was hard for me to understand what she was saying. Then she suddenly stopped and, her arms motionless at her sides, began slowly all over again. "How old are you, Granddad?"

He seemed relieved at the change of pace. "I'm fifty-seven," he said. Anything over fifty is old in China.

"Tell me about yourself."

He looked worried again, and, wetting his lips, started talking. He had worked in Tientsin, he told her, until he was fifteen and had then been sent to Kalgan as an apprentice in the fur-curing business. He had stayed there three or maybe four years, and after that taken a better position as a journeyman in Peking. The following year he had married. He and his growing family had lived in many cities, and his story was long, and complicated by dates and calculations of how old he had been at various times and places. His story, begun in the last days of the Ch'ing dynasty, was a history of bandits, revolutions, warlords, and foreign aggression, and through it all were woven the same themes—escape from poverty, from war, from death.

When he finished, the young-old girl began swinging her arms again. "And now you do a little speculating in flour?" she asked.

"Yes."

"How many days have you been in Peking?"

"Three."

"But you forgot to register with the police?"

"Yes."

The room was silent. The swinging moved from her arms into her body, and she rocked back and forth on her heels. "Where were you when you were thirty-two?" she asked. "Answer quickly!"

"Tientsin," he said.

"You said you were in Tientsin from the ninth to the thirteenth year of the Republic. You left there when you were thirty-one. What happened in the fourteenth year, when you said you were in Peking?" She had an excellent memory, and she pinpointed ages and dates until her victim was hopelessly contradicting himself every time he spoke. They even got back into the sixteenth year of the reign of Kuang Hsu, the next-to-last Manchu emperor, and, from time to time, used Gregorian-calendar dates as well.

She continued to fire one question after another at the old man, who by now was stuttering and sheepishly grinning from ear to ear, and bowing up and down in rhythm with her questioning. Whether he was guilty of anything serious or not (this was obviously just the preliminary softening up), I couldn't tell. She had certainly succeeded in making a liar out of him, and, leaving him bowed and red of face, she turned to a girl nursing a baby. "What a lovable baby!" she exclaimed. "Tell me something about yourself, little sister." And the performance started over again.

I almost hoped she would ask me some questions, but she had probably decided that a foreigner was more than she cared to tackle, and she never even looked in my direction. Instead, at ten minutes past seven one of the officers phoned the Central Department of Public Safety, and it was confirmed that I was a registered foreigner who had declared himself a resident of exactly the place where they found me that night. No questions were asked me, no apology was given—just "You may go now," and, walking home with Aimee in the bright morning sunshine, I became angry for the first time.

It was flattering to discover that several of Aimee's sisters, and even old Aunt Chin—having been informed by our gateman that I was about to be released—were waiting at our main gate to welcome me safely home. While we were all standing just inside the gate and Aimee was explaining about the telephone call to the Department of Public Safety, two old ladies and two old men came into view on the road outside. The four of them carried brooms and, keeping their faces down, were engaged somewhat less than wholeheartedly in sweeping the road.

"Isn't that Mme. Wang and her husband?" Aunt Chin asked, in a startled voice. I could see only their backs, but one of the women did look like our neighbor. "It *is* Mme. Wang!" Aunt Chin exclaimed. "And that's her brother and sister-in-law!"

She immediately hurried out to speak to them, but the Wangs, still with their heads down, only swept the harder. "Mme. Wang!" Aunt Chin shouted. "What are you doing?"

"Please," Mme. Wang said, without looking up, "don't stop us," and her pale face flushed. "We have to do this." She was apparently too choked with emotion to say more, and her husband finished for her.

"We've been ordered to sweep the road every morning for twenty days," he said. "It's our punishment, and we mustn't stop to talk."

Too stunned to protest, Aunt Chin let the Wangs move off down the street. In a minute, one of the Wang serving maids, who had been following them at a distance, came along carrying a thermos jug, and stopped to tell us what had happened.

Her master and mistress, she said, had been playing a simple game of mah-jongg late last night with their relatives—they thought nobody would really object, because they weren't playing for money—when suddenly the house was raided and they were caught with the tiles in their hands. If the Wangs didn't need to sleep at night like honest working folk, the police had said sarcastically, then the Wangs shouldn't mind sweeping the neighborhood streets in the morning as a token of their willingness to make themselves useful to the community. And they were sentenced on the spot. When the maid had told us this, she hurried off down the street after

143

her master and mistress, ready, I supposed, to give aid and comfort from her thermos jug.

Aunt Chin and Auntie Hu had prepared a big breakfast in celebration of my return, and despite the fact that I had been eating steadily all through the night and needed food a good deal less than sleep, Aimee and I went with them to their rooms. While we had breakfast, Aunt Chin talked. "It *was* the Night People you saw last night," she said bitterly. "They were everywhere in the neighborhood, and that's how they caught poor Mme. Wang and her husband playing mah-jongg—not even for money. How wrong life is! It may not be generally known now, but, as a girl, Mme. Wang was famous for her delicate beauty."

We were still sitting over breakfast when our gateman brought in a letter from the local police. Aimee read it to me, her eyes growing round. It demanded a written apology from me for the crime of failing to register, and said that such high-handed tactics, employed by imperialist-minded foreigners and other leftover reactionaries and enemies of the people, could no longer be tolerated in the New China, and so on. It was clear what the police wanted—simply something to incriminate every foreigner, and particularly every American, if not in one way, then in another, for possible future use.

Aimee and I negotiated with the police for two days before we realized that they were determined to make me admit my "guilt" in writing. If I continued to refuse, it was, I knew, quite possible that they would arrange to find a gun concealed in my room, or a secret code book, or plans to assassinate Mao Tse-tung. Aimee and I decided that it would be wiser to accept the lesser guilt and be done with it. She wrote out a terse apology and I signed it. The police accepted it, stamped my papers accordingly, and returned them to me.

As the days passed with no further trouble, I began to see

what I had accomplished by surrendering. My misdemeanor became a kind of decoration on my various passes and permits, and, in all my encounters with officialdom in which these papers were shown, was the chief object of interest. Those who saw it seemed relieved that my guilt had already been established and that it was unnecessary to devise means to incriminate me further. They always smilingly returned the papers and politely sent me on my way. My new criminal record was really a great convenience. But although life in the Yu mansion seemed to go on just as it had in the past, and the walls were as high as ever, the rooms as quiet, the halls as cool, and the garden as vast, I had lost my peace of mind.

The members of the Yu family must have sensed my feeling, because suddenly—or so it seemed to me—they began to treat me with unusual consideration. Some of them even brought around tasty dishes specially prepared for me. And in the street I got the impression that people were being kind to me (not because they liked Americans so much more than other foreigners but because the Communist government liked Americans so much less). Pedicab men, as soon as they discovered I was an American, pumped harder, speeding me to my destination; dealers often reduced their prices; and once, in a moment of candor, a pro-Communist student of William Empson's confessed to me, "When the Americans were here, we wanted them to go, but now that they have really gone, with their music, their movies, and their money, we rather miss them."

Meanwhile, Aunt Chin wrapped her mah-jongg sets in copies of the *China People's Newspaper* and packed them away in the bottom of a chest, and though the family tried to find another dog to take the place of old Baldy, there were none for sale, and even the strays had disappeared.

HOUSES AND PEOPLE
AND TABLES AND CHAIRS

OLD MR. YU left my wife and her two brothers and eight sisters the joint owners of the Yu family mansion. At the same time, they inherited the family's ancestral temple and the Yu family burial plot.

This was only a small part, Aimee told me, of what her family had owned when she was a girl. There had been villas and farming land in the country, other houses in the city, and, above all, gold—bars, cups, chains, and bracelets of gold in a multitude of sizes, and the bulk of it in one-ounce boat-shaped ingots, sometimes called "shoes," since they resembled the small silk shoes worn by Chinese women with bound feet. In Aimee's youth, all this gold had been kept in the Peking mansion (neither banks nor paper money were to be trusted), concealed in pots under the floor tiles and courtyard flagstones, or hidden in secret recesses within the walls; and it would all still be there, Aimee lamented, had her father not been such a staunch patriot.

When, about 1934, the government asked all Chinese citizens to turn their private hoards of gold into national currency to help resist the Japanese aggressors, Mr. Yu had piled all the gold he could find into his horse carriage (he owned an automobile but refused to ride in it) and taken it off to a central bank, where the amazed president had converted it into freshly printed one-hundred-yuan bills. The habits of tradition were not entirely disregarded, though, because old Mr. Yu had carried the new bills back home again for safekeeping.

This move, however, was to no avail. As a result of inflation and the advance of the Japanese, the bills had been abruptly withdrawn from circulation within two years, leaving Mr. Yu a poorer but wiser patriot.

Through the years, the Yu children from time to time had found, at the bottoms of old chests and in the backs of drawers, reminders of their father's folly. I found some, too, in our suite of rooms. One day, I came across a cache of faded notes, and on another occasion I discovered a pack of a hundred yellowed bills still bound in their original wrapper. Even if the bills had been negotiable, it would have taken, considering the value of the yuan in 1949, a trunkful of them to buy one good meal in a Peking restaurant. All that remained of the family gold was a bracelet or two and a few shoes that had either been overlooked by Mr. Yu or had been held out by other members of the family.

On his deathbed, Mr. Yu had felt it necessary to assure his children that they were not destitute. There was no reason that the house could not go on protecting them and their children and their grandchildren, he had told them, and if they sold their antiques one by one, as need arose, they and generations after them could live comfortably in the old mansion without troubles or worries. "Though I have made mistakes," he had said, "I can die knowing I have done well by you all." He had referred to the enormous collection of porcelains, rare bronzes, and fine old paintings that the family had accumulated over the years, as much out of the love of a sound investment as a love of beauty.

The Yu children had tearfully thanked their father for his thoughtfulness. They had not pointed out to him that the house in which he was dying might very well be confiscated in lieu of the new taxes being imposed by the Communist government. They had also not mentioned the fact that antique Ming furniture, for example, was being sold by weight on the open market as firewood, that porcelains, bronzes, and paintings, whether fine or otherwise, symbolized in the New China a class slated for extermination, and that no one in his right mind would have dreamed of buying the very objects that would single him out for the exterminators.

The house itself, while beautiful, was old and in poor condition. The walls, made of brick and mortar, were perhaps the things most urgently in need of repair. In several parts of the house, supporting pillars had given way and the great weight of the roofs rested directly on the walls. Cracks had appeared, and the back wall of old Aunt Chin's sitting room had begun to bulge ominously.

"That wall isn't going to go on standing forever," Aunt Chin was saying to Elder Brother one spring afternoon in 1950 when Aimee and I entered her sitting room. She and Auntie Hu had invited us for a game of bridge, and we sat down to wait while Aunt Chin finished her conversation. "I know it's going to fall down, because my cats won't go near it," she went on, lighting an asthma cigarette. "Cats are intelligent, and they don't do anything without a reason."

"I'm sure of *that*," Elder Brother said.

Aunt Chin then asked me to help Elder Brother move a desk away from the back wall. Mystified, he did this, and uncovered a small recess in the wall. It was empty.

"That hole is one of the reasons why this wall is weaker than the others," Aunt Chin said. "There used to be a cabinet with a concealed door in its back standing here, but it was too big for the room, and I took it away. Anyway, the hole was never a very safe place to hide gold."

Elder Brother agreed that the wall was probably weaker than the others in the mansion, but what could he do, he asked, and explained that the family simply didn't have enough money to make repairs and pay taxes at the same time. Under a new monthly levy introduced by the Communists, houses were being taxed by size on an increasing scale; that is, the larger the house, the more disproportionately large the tax.

Since the Yu mansion was so huge, the tax reached—for the impoverished Yu clan, anyway—a staggering sum.

"There isn't much use in paying taxes on a house that's falling down." Aunt Chin sniffed. "I've told you more times than I can remember that I have the money to help make repairs on this house. I have ten ounces of gold here now that I'll be happy to give you. It should more than cover the cost of repairing this wall and some of the rest of the house as well."

"We don't want your gold," Elder Brother insisted. "You are my father's sister-in-law, and you have been here all these years since your husband's death, as our family guest. It would be highly improper for us to use your money now. We are more than honored that you have consented to make your home with us."

"Don't tell me that again," Aunt Chin said crossly, starting to shuffle a pack of cards. "Just remember, I warned you, and don't blame me when the wall falls down."

"Thank you," Elder Brother said, bowing himself out of the room. "Thank you very much."

I felt sorry for him. As the new head of the family, he bore a great responsibility, and though the house tax was bad enough, he also had to contend with a new land tax. Laid out four hundred years before, the mansion proper sprawled around seven tiled courtyards interconnected by an extensive network of roofed and balustraded promenades, ending to the west in the vast walled garden.

This garden, which, though unkempt, was in its prime, possessed a beauty not matched elsewhere in the house. And so, when it finally became clear, that spring, that the house must be sold to avoid being confiscated at the inevitable time when the family would no longer be able to pay the taxes, the prospect of losing the garden hurt more deeply than anything else.

Late one afternoon, I was sitting in the garden's ruined Pavilion of Harmonious Virtues. Nothing much was left but a square stone foundation surrounded by a balustrade. The rest of it—the few unbroken roof tiles, the pillars and beams and carved woodwork—had been heaped into a neat pile close up under the garden wall. I was looking at the inscription on a slab of stone standing nearby when Elder Brother, who had quietly come up behind me, asked, "Can you read it?"

The twelve characters of the inscription were not difficult, and I read them aloud, " 'Stone not speak, but know all. Man not move, but do all.' "

"Very good," he said, beaming at me. "Fourth Sister found a truly intelligent husband."

"Where did this stone come from?" I asked.

"It came from South China, and six months were required to bring it up the Grand Canal by barge," Elder Brother said. "Most of the stones in this garden have been carried here from places thousands of miles away. In the old days, when cultured people still appreciated them, some of these stones were worth almost as much as the house itself."

There were stones of every type, shape, and size in the garden. The more fantastic ones were lavalike, gray-blue and green, filled with holes and hollowed into whirls and arabesques by wind and water. They bordered the now empty pool of the garden and were heaped up in piles that looked from a distance as huge and wild as primeval mountains. Other stones, taller than I, were balanced on slender ends, like sculptured maidens on tiptoe. The least fanciful were long, striated gray shafts of stone that shot straight up out of the earth. These were the rarest, Elder Brother told me, and had great strength, for there was more stone below ground than above. "They are called living stones, because it is believed that they grow an inch every hundred years," he said.

"Stones *move*?" I asked.

Elder Brother laughed. "They do, and trees walk," he said.

"Have you noticed the grove of old cedars at the west end of the garden?" I had noticed the cedars. Twisted and bent with age, some ten of them were huddled close together. "They are the oldest things here," Elder Brother went on. "They were here before the house was built or this garden laid out. There are no records left, but my father told me that they were in the courtyard of a temple that once stood here and burned down during the reign of the third Ming emperor. It is said that those trees, wiser and older than holy men and hermits, sometimes walk at night, in the dark of the moon. I haven't seen them walking myself, but Aunt Chin will tell you they do. I believed it when I was a child, and never dared go near them, but now I have come to like those wise old trees better than anything else in the garden."

I asked Elder Brother what he thought would happen to the rocks and trees after the house was sold, and he looked suddenly pained. "Nothing will happen to them," he said severely. "We will not sell the house to anyone who doesn't promise to keep the garden just as it is now."

Early one evening a few days later, Aimee and I, lured by the sound of music, joined several of her sisters on one of the verandas facing the garden. The sisters had brought out an old hand-cranked gramophone and were playing a recording of Handel's "Messiah." At the same time, they were carrying on a loud conversation. "Can't we at least take the peonies?" Ninth Sister asked.

"How can we take the peonies without taking the chrysanthemums and the wisteria and the plum trees, too?" another sister asked. "How is it possible to take anything without taking everything?"

"And I want to take the pools," Ninth Sister continued. "I can remember when I was a little girl, the pools were full of water, and great golden fish swam at the bottom. They looked so cool and far away. What happened to all those fish?"

"Someone probably ate them," one of her sisters answered.

"The pools are no use, anyway," another sister said, changing the record and rewinding the machine. The garden resounded to the opening of the "Hallelujah Chorus." "It's illegal now to have any water at all in a private garden. The Russians are afraid of mosquitoes." Shortly after the Chinese Communists had captured Peking, Russian advisers arrived to assist in the construction of a Communist China. Because the Russians had complained that mosquitoes were a menace to health, the Chinese authorities, despite the fact that malaria was unheard of in Peking, had dredged out the city's ancient lakes, destroying the thousands of lotus plants, and covered the rock-lined shores with smoothly undulating concrete, until each lake had come to look almost as placidly uninteresting as a modern yacht basin. Simultaneously, the government had instituted a house-to-house campaign to fill in or cover all pools, wells, and streams in private gardens.

"Don't you have mosquitoes in America?" Ninth Sister asked me, and I told her that we did.

"Then why aren't there any mosquitoes in Russia?" she asked. The Russians had given the impression that mosquitoes had been virtually exterminated in their own country.

"Of course there are mosquitoes in Russia," one of the older sisters shouted over the hallelujahs. "They only want us to think they're better than we are."

The record came to an end. "They're no better than I am," Ninth Sister muttered to herself, "and I *like* mosquitoes." Her sisters, who were busy packing up the phonograph and records, paid no attention to her. "Anyway," she finished emphatically, stepping off the veranda into the garden, "I like goldfish!"

During the summer of 1950, I became used to innumerable groups of people being led in and out of the suite of rooms in which Aimee and I lived. Both the men and the women of these groups were invariably dressed in the blue cotton jackets and trousers so popular in the New China, and the groups themselves usually represented some governmental department or labor union in search of anything from extra office space to a place for a day nursery. At the time of such visits, I would try to make myself as inconspicuous as possible, in order to avoid the lengthy explanations a foreigner's presence in the house would entail. I would sit in a small alcove off our sitting room, behind a silk-backed lattice partition of carved grapevines, out of which peeped bats and squirrels. I was rarely discovered.

Peking has a short rainy season, in early summer. One gray afternoon toward the end of this season, when the rains had stopped at midday, though the eaves continued to drip, a contingent of possible buyers toured the house, and I took my customary place in the alcove with a book open on my lap. After a while, I could hear voices and then the sound of people moving about on the other side of the silk partition. "This is the Eastern Study," I heard Aimee say. "It contains our library."

A man spoke. "Your house is really big," he said. "But we don't need so many rooms."

Someone asked if there were any water outlets, and Aimee answered that there were.

"Then we could make this room into a laundry," the first man said. "We could put sinks against those walls and cut down those trees outside the windows to make the room brighter."

I didn't like this idea at all and was pleased to hear Aimee say that the trees were old and valuable and that it would be a shame to cut them down. At the other end of the house, she told them, there was another building and courtyard, which would make a much better laundry. "Let me show you," she said. There was a bustle of moving people, and the voices faded away.

I waited a while and then put down my book and looked out. The sitting room was empty. Crossing it, I stepped out onto the terrace just in time to hear a rumble and clatter from someplace in the rear of the house. The noise lasted three or four seconds, and then, after a short silence, there was the sound of excited voices.

After some hesitation, because the buyers were still in the house, I started off to see what had happened, and had gone halfway down the flagstoned gallery leading to the rear courtyards when I met Third Sister's little boy running toward me. "What happened?" I asked.

"The house is falling down!" he yelled, and passed without stopping.

In a few moments, I met Aimee, coming at a slower pace from the same direction. "What happened?" I asked again.

"The back wall of Aunt Chin's sitting room just fell down," she said.

I pictured Aunt Chin buried under tons of bricks. "Is she all right?" I asked.

"Oh, she's fine," Aimee said. "She's still playing solitaire. We were taking the buyers through the courtyard behind her rooms when suddenly there was a big noise, and the whole wall fell right down in front of us, and there was Aunt Chin sitting inside at her card table and playing solitaire as calmly as if nothing at all had happened."

"What did the buyers do?" I asked.

"Fifth Sister is seeing them off at the gate now. They said they had no idea the house was in such bad condition. It's too humiliating."

Aimee turned and we walked on to Aunt Chin's courtyard. Most of the family was there ahead of us, milling about inside her rooms and out. At first I couldn't see her, and then when I did, I found that Aimee had been right. She was sitting at her card table, and at the same time giving directions to one and all.

"That old radio of mine is under there somewhere," she said, indicating the collapsed wall, "but it doesn't matter. I never listened to it, anyway."

"Didn't you have a desk sitting against the wall?" one of the sisters asked.

"Yes, I did," Aunt Chin answered, "and there is something in one of the drawers I would like to have, too." I could see chair legs sticking out of the rubble at the back of the room, but the radio and desk were nowhere visible. I walked over to the open space and looked out into the back courtyard, where there was an even larger pile of rubble. Second Sister and her four young sons were there, poking about among the bricks. This was the second part of the Yu mansion to collapse since I lived there. It looked like the start of an ominous pattern.

"Do you think there's danger of these other walls falling?" I asked the eldest son. He said he didn't think so. He said one reason the back wall had fallen was that some of the roof tiles above it were missing, so that the water, instead of draining off, had seeped down into the wall until, thoroughly soaked after weeks of rain, the mortar had finally given way.

"Madame Wang's book of Long Life Elixir Recipes is in that desk drawer," Aunt Chin said. "I borrowed it from her last week, and she'll be wanting it back."

Second Sister, looking in through the space where the wall had stood, said, "We can get that out, at least." She turned to her sons. "Surely the four of you can find the desk." It seemed absurd to search for a book of Long Life Elixir Recipes at just that moment, but because there was nothing much more practical any of us could do, we sat down and waited while Second Sister's sons dug among the bricks. Someone brought them a shovel, and after a while one of them called out, "We've found it!"

Aunt Chin got up and walked over to them. "That's not the desk. That's the top of the radio," she said. Then all of us except the four sons settled down again and someone made tea. It almost seemed to be a party.

"What kind of recipes are in that book?" Fifth Sister asked.

"They're quite impossible," Aunt Chin said. "They all call for freshly fallen cones from a five-needled pine tree, which must be gathered either at dawn or at sundown. That isn't too difficult, I suppose, but the other herbs and berries named in the recipes simply can't be found nowadays. It's unfortunate, too, because the book guarantees that if the recipes are followed exactly, elixir pills can be made that prolong life many years." Most of the family tolerantly considered Aunt Chin's interest in such matters as part of her old-fashioned charm; a credulous few took everything she said as the purest gospel.

I was drinking a second cup of tea, when one of the sons called in to us, "We found it, again."

Aunt Chin looked out once more. "That's it," she said. "The book is in the top right drawer." There was a sound of ripping wood, and in a few moments the book, looking disappointingly ordinary, was passed in to Aunt Chin.

"Don't you want these, too?" the boy asked, offering Aunt Chin a handful of what appeared to be shoes of gold.

"Aunt Chin!" someone exclaimed. "Why didn't you tell us you had gold in the desk? Don't you think that's more important than Madame Wang's book?"

"This isn't my gold," Aunt Chin protested. "The little I have is in the bedroom. I never saw these pieces of gold before. They certainly weren't in the desk."

"That's right," the boy said. "They're just scattered around out here."

"Is it real gold?" someone asked. Aunt Chin weighed a piece in her hand, while Elder Brother pressed his thumbnail into another. The pieces were pure gold, they declared.

By noon next day, it was decided, amid much rejoicing, that the shoes of gold—there were nine altogether—had been a forgotten cache of old Mr. Yu's, or perhaps even of some earlier ancestor's, which had lain concealed all these years in some chamber of the wall other than the empty one Elder Brother and I saw before the wall fell. And no wonder it fell, everybody said, because in doing so it had yielded up, at the last moment, a treasure that rightfully belonged to the mansion. It was unanimously agreed that the gold should be used to help pay the cost of repainting the main gates and buildings, making broken roof tiles and rotten beams whole again, and re-erecting the garden pavilion and, of course, the wall itself.

During the first weeks following the rainy season, there was great activity in the mansion as carpenters were followed by masons, and masons by tile-setters, and tile-setters by painters who, day by day, slowly restored to the faded pillars and balustrades the fresh glitter of colors—in particular, a beautiful vermilion of great clearness and depth—that no member of the family had ever thought to see again. When the last touches of gold and turquoise and peacock blue were added to the bracketing under the outspreading eaves, the work was completed and the house was transformed into a palace of old, through whose glittering courts we wandered bedazzled by the miracle we ourselves had brought about. But our raptures were soon cut short. Perhaps because the old house had become so beautiful that no one could resist it, or perhaps for some more utilitarian reason, the Yu mansion was sold the week following the renovation, and the Yu family was given one month to vacate.

The Ministry of Finance bought the house. (The Communists could, of course, have simply appropriated the mansion, but in the big cities, at least, they went through legal channels. At that time, 1950, two years after the Communists had taken control, the government was less secure and hesitated, in centers of culture and tradition such as Peking, to estrange China's old intellectual class completely. The horrors of the Cultural Revolution still lay fifteen years in the future.) The price paid the Yu family was the yuan equivalent of fifteen thousand dollars. At any time previously, this would have been only a fraction of the true value of the mansion, but in 1950 it was a good price, and the Yu children considered themselves fortunate to have got so much. They were told that Po I-po, the minister of finance himself, intended to use the house as a city residence, and they were further assured that the rocks and trees of the garden would be cared for just as they had been in the past.

Within the month, both Elder Brother and Second Brother bought small, two-courtyard houses in the eastern part of Peking, and offered to take in First, Fifth, Eighth, and Ninth Sisters, who were all unmarried. Elder Brother invited Aunt Chin to make her home with him, too, but she refused, saying the house would be too small and that both she and her cats were too old to learn to live under other people's feet. Instead, she told the family, she was moving to a temple in the countryside near Peking, to which her husband had made large donations during his life, with the understanding that any member of his immediate family would always be welcomed there.

Aunt Chin and Auntie Hu were the first to leave. She had given most of her heavy furniture away to various members of the family, and as she sat waiting in a pedicab, an old knitted hat pulled tight around her head, with her cats in a basket at her feet, she looked old and poorer and sadder than I had ever seen her before. Just as she left, she leaned out and pushed a shoe of gold into my hand. "I saved this for you," she said. "You and your wife must promise to come and visit me. No one in the country will be able to play cards."

That night, I showed Aimee the gold and told her what Aunt Chin had said. Aimee looked at it carefully. "Aunt Chin had ten ounces of gold. I remember, because she tried to give it to Elder Brother that afternoon in her room, before the wall collapsed," Aimee said. "If she says she saved one ounce for you, that means she must have already used nine ounces. Then the nine ounces of gold the boys found after the wall fell down must have been hers, and she must have put it in that hole behind the desk so that it would be found if the wall ever did fall down." It seemed a logical enough explanation for the all too fortuitous presence of the gold in the wall, and when the story was told to Elder Brother, he agreed that Aunt Chin had had her own way, after all.

Second Sister and her husband and children were the next to leave, amid a fever of packing and tears. They had decided to join her husband's family at Wuhan, in Central China, where he had been offered work. Sixth Sister, married to an agricultural engineer, was moving to a research farm near Peking, while Seventh and Third Sisters both bought small houses in the city. Aimee and I were to live with Second Brother until we completed arrangements to leave China. Aimee, of course, intended to travel to America with me. We looked forward to discovering what a society endowed with human rights and personal freedoms would make possible for us. We had already applied for exit permits, and I had started making inquiries about ships to Hong Kong. Almost every day someone left, and there always seemed to be a horse cart or two at the main gate being loaded with personal belongings.

We would all have felt a good deal sadder about the breakup if we had not been so busy. On top of everything else, there was the division of the family porcelains, bronzes, paintings, furniture, and jewelry. Since Aimee and I intended to take with us as many as we could of the smaller objects of her share (one-eleventh of the total contents of the house), we had the additional task of making quintuple lists for presentation to customs on leaving China. A tentative listing of the contents of only one of a pair of red lacquer chests included, among other things: five bronze incense burners, twenty-five ink sticks (five with pearls), six mounted fans, eight unmounted fans, two cut-velvet jackets, one yellow silk gown, six brocade strips, two bolts of gold-and-purple silk, and thirteen black-and-white paintings (Ming).

When the main body of the furniture at last began to move, carts departed from the street gate day after day in an endless train, loaded with cabinets, books, chests, candlesticks, lamps, bric-a-brac, stoves, mirrors, carpets, tables, and chairs—the almost overwhelming accumulation of four centuries. Practically as much was discarded or sold by weight out the back door as was carted away from the front, and still, as the days passed, the flow seemed only to increase.

Elder Brother estimated that some two hundred horse-drawn cartloads left the house in the space of two weeks. Then, one day, Second Brother and those of us who were to go with him found that the house was nearly empty. Several chairs and tables, our beds, our clothes, and a few cooking utensils and dishes were all that was left, and it was time for us, too, to go. At that moment, in the sudden quiet, we thought of the house, its rooms vacant, its doors and gates standing ajar, waiting, it seemed, for some final clarifying gesture to be made. But there was no gesture. We simply left, one after another, in pedicabs following the carts loaded with our personal belongings, and the great double doors of the main gate were closed after us by the ministry's new caretaker, who had already moved into the gatehouse. I never saw the mansion again.

Bound for the new house on the other side of the city in East-Kuan Yin Temple Lane, our little cavalcade of beds and dishes and pots and pans seemed a poor ending as we crossed, at twilight, the great marble bridge spanning the waterway between the imperial North and Central Sea lakes. Strings of electric lights outlined the palaces beside the north shore, and, to the south, red flags whipped in the wind over palaces that were now converted into government offices. Spotlights played on the black waters, and the music of a military band blared through loudspeakers from the far shore. But despite all this, some part of the old splendor still remained, and I felt, with a sudden lightening of the heart, that the Yu mansion, the lakes, and the ancient city itself shared a resiliency and a strength to do battle with whatever time and fate had in store for them.

That night, we had our first meal in the new house (four small units around a central courtyard) and retired early, but it was hot and not easy to sleep. The floors creaked under the unaccustomed weight of the great purple sandalwood tables and chairs brought from the old mansion, and a pair of huge cabinets towered menacingly over the foot of the bed. I heard Second Brother cough on the other side of the courtyard and in a house nearby a baby was crying.

It seemed hard to imagine that anything of the old way of life could survive here. As the days passed and a routine established itself in our new surroundings, I found that the Yu family had been a very delicate thing, after all, and that it had been the old house that had given the Yu children so much of their identity.

One day, about a month after we had left the Yu mansion, Fifth Sister went back to ask permission to dig up a few of the exceptionally fine white chrysanthemums in the old garden so she could plant them in the tiny courtyard of Elder Brother's new house. We all waited impatiently at home to hear what she would have to tell us of her visit. So far as I know, she was the only one of the Yu family ever to see the house again.

Fifth Sister came home in tears. Her face was swollen and

ugly from crying, and though she was close to hysteria, we were able slowly to piece together what had happened both to her and to the house. From the very beginning, Fifth Sister's story made clear, the Ministry of Finance had not intended to use the house as a private residence, but in order to gain possession of it as quickly as possible had simply promised whatever seemed likely at the time to satisfy the Yu family. The house, she told us, had been converted into a private hospital clinic for employees of the ministry. The brilliant colors we had restored to the doors, the pillars, and the balustrades had disappeared under thick layers of whitewash, and the great halls had been partitioned into rows of cubbyholes, each containing a white bed, a white wardrobe, a white table, and a white chair. At least, I thought, the mansion had been able to make a compromise with the New China, and in its altered form, as a servant of the people, it survived. It was the fate of the garden that filled us with horror and disbelief.

The garden was simply gone, Fifth Sister told us. Its miniature hills had been pushed back into the pools from which they had been excavated centuries before. The rebuilt Pavilion of Harmonious Virtues had been dismantled, the trees and shrubs had been cut down and uprooted, the ornamental rocks had been crushed and leveled with the earth, the shafts of living stone had been severed at their bases, and the grove of ancient cedars had been chopped away. In short, the wild and lovely garden had become an open lot where the Ministry of Finance now parked its trucks. There had been no white flowers for Fifth Sister, although the new occupants had been eager and proud to let her see the expanse of pulverized stone and raw earth where the garden had stood, and these same new owners had been honestly amazed to see Fifth Sister's grief in the face of so much genuine progress.

None of us had much to say to one another at dinner that evening, and we ate little of the pale, oily food that Elder

Sister, who was in charge of the kitchen, had taken all afternoon to prepare. Fifth Sister mumbled something to herself about committing suicide and being done with it. I slept poorly that night and awoke, to the sound of wind and rain, thinking about Aunt Chin. It seemed suddenly urgent that Aimee and I visit her, if for no other reason than to find out by just what form of defeat she, too, had been overtaken.

The next morning dawned clear and warm, although the storm of the night before had left a touch of autumn in the air. Aimee seemed as eager as I to visit Aunt Chin, and after a hasty breakfast we boarded the public bus bound for the terminal outside the gate of the Summer Palace where we hired pedicabs to take us on to Aunt Chin's temple in the countryside. This temple was not a famous one or, for that matter, a real temple at all, Aimee told me, because most of its monks were aging eunuchs who had been ejected from the palace after the fall of the Manchu dynasty and simply had been too loyal, or too timid, to move very far away.

In some fifteen minutes, we arrived at the temple and dismissed our pedicabs. Several tall pine trees grew close beside the temple's dilapidated main gate, and its stone steps were strewn with needles and pinecones that had fallen in the storm. Picking our way through them, we found an old man inside the gate who, when we questioned him, offered to lead us to Aunt Chin's quarters. His wrinkled face looked curiously soft and hairless, and I wondered if he was a eunuch. He led us through a series of courts, none of them in very good condition, past a central prayer hall with a yellow tiled roof indicating imperial patronage, through a gate of faded turquoise, and into a side courtyard filled with what looked like the remains of a vegetable garden. At the north end of the garden, its white-papered windows facing south, stood a neat building containing perhaps three rooms, and, to

163

its side, a kind of greenhouse. Next to this greenhouse was a grove of thorny bushes.

"Is anyone home?" Aimee called, after the old man had left us.

There was a sudden rustling of thorny branches, and Aunt Chin, looking somewhat dishevelled and carrying a pan of small yellow berries, pushed herself into view. "You've come," she said to us.

"We've come," Aimee answered.

Aunt Chin asked about us and other members of the family, and we gave her what news we had, but we said nothing then about the old mansion. Later, we all sat down to lunch in Aunt Chin's sitting room, which she had furnished with her own tables and chairs. Although I remembered them well from the mansion, they looked as if they had sat in that room for many years. Aunt Chin had hung three paintings on the wall; far from being the elaborate blue-and-green palace-filled landscapes she had displayed in the old house, these were of a pomegranate on a branch, a pair of crabs, and a sleeping cat.

Auntie Hu carried our food over from the temple's main kitchen. As long as we were in a Buddhist temple, Aunt Chin said, it was only proper that we eat a Buddhist vegetarian meal. We were served mushrooms and tree ears (a kind of fungus) and bean curd, and there were pickled plums, and lotus seeds boiled in sugar water, and eggs cured in lime, and, as a last course, caramelized sweet potatoes.

While Aimee and I, who had been enduring Elder Sister's cooking, ate as if we had forgotten the taste of food, Aunt Chin, looking surprisingly well, talked about her new life. "This used to be an herb garden," she said, indicating the garden outside the windows. "During the dynasty it supplied medicinal herbs to the palace. Did you notice that I have begun to recultivate the plots nearest the house?" I had noticed when we came in that some dandelionlike weeds were growing in neat rows near the doorstep, but it hadn't occurred to me that they were herbs, and it certainly hadn't occurred to me that Aunt Chin was cultivating them. "The monk who tended this garden is very old," Aunt Chin went on, "and spends most of his time these days in the Buddha Hall—'meditating,' he says—but I've persuaded him to teach me all he can remember about herbs. He gave me his old herb and medicine books, too, since he doesn't use them any more, and he gave me the original chart of the garden. Wait, I'll show you."

Aunt Chin bustled into a side room and came back in a moment with a large roll of stiff paper, which she opened on the desk. The paper was divided into squares and rectangles, each containing a picture of the sun and a crescent moon, with numbers and various mysterious-looking symbols under them. "This is a planting chart," she said. "It will take me several years, but with the help of this and the old monk and the books, I think I can replant much of the garden."

"But why do you want to do that?" Aimee objected. "It's too much work for you, and who wants all those herbs, anyway?"

"People seem to go on dying just as they always did, in spite of all the modern chemical medicines they keep stuffing into themselves," Aunt Chin said. "My herbs may not keep people alive, but they won't kill them. The villagers hereabouts will use them, and certainly the temple will, and I'll enjoy drinking my own herb teas, whether anyone else does or not!"

I was astounded. Aunt Chin was an asthmatic old woman nearing the end of her life. Gossip and cards and cats had been her only occupation for years, and yet here she was, ejected from her home, thrust into a world strange and, I would have guessed, inhospitable to her, learning what looked to me very much like a new trick.

The time had come, I decided, to tell her what had happened to the Peking house and garden. When I finished, she looked neither saddened nor surprised.

"It *is* too bad that the garden is gone," she said. "It was very beautiful, but it was an old garden. The house was old, too," she added. I waited for her to go on, but that was apparently all she intended to say.

"You did leave the gold in the wall, didn't you?" I asked.

A patch of sunlight had moved across Aunt Chin's face, and she put up her hand to shield her eyes. "*I* didn't give up the gold," she said. "The wall did. I only let things go their own way. Houses and people and tables and chairs move and change of themselves, following destinies that cannot be altered. When things change into other things or lose themselves or destroy themselves, there is nothing we can do but let them go."

Aunt Chin must have felt that she had said all we needed to hear, because she abruptly moved on to another subject by instructing Auntie Hu to clear the table for bridge. It would be a sad waste not to take advantage of a foursome gathered under her own roof, she told us. Later, while we played, she chattered away as volubly and cheerfully as ever, but did not mention the house again. It was near sundown when we finished the final rubber and Aimee and I prepared to start back to Peking. There would be no pedicabs outside, and we would have to walk to the bus stop.

Aunt Chin looked at me. "I may not see you again," she said, "and gold is a poor gift to remember me by. Bring me some hot water and a little of that new herb tea. I want to serve our guests," Aunt Chin instructed her companion, who hurried away. Aunt Chin turned to me and said, "I want to tell you one last story, which I have never told anyone before, about the woman we call Auntie Hu." She paused and then began. "Fifty years ago when the allied troops occupied Peking after the Boxer Rebellion, Auntie Hu, then a little girl, saw her own mother bayonetted to death by a foreign soldier."

At that moment, Auntie Hu returned with the tea and hot water and watched as Aunt Chin placed the tea into a pot and then poured in the hot water. "Put the rest of the tea in a jar and wait for me at the temple gate," Aunt Chin said to her.

After Auntie Hu left, Aunt Chin continued, "From that day to this, she has never spoken a word, and I have taken care of her all these years, nurturing her pain as my own. But I see now that we have been wrong to hold too long in our hearts the evil of others."

I drank the tea. "The taste is bitter," Aunt Chin said, "but it cleans the blood."

Aimee drank too, and after a few minutes Aunt Chin walked with us to the outer steps of the temple's main gate where Auntie Hu waited with the jar of tea. The first breeze of evening, cool with the scent of pine and the coming autumn, stirred the straight gray fringes of Aunt Chin's hair. She took the jar of tea from Auntie Hu, who seemed about to cry, and put it into my hands.

There was nothing more to say except to thank them and bid them good-bye. After we had walked a little way down the road, we turned to wave, but they did not see us. They were down on their hands and knees busily gathering up the scattered pinecones.

Two months later, our exit visas came through and Aimee and I left China, presumably never to see it again.

A GIFT OF NEW VASES

IN AUGUST 1981, as the director of a school in Kyoto teaching the arts of Japan and armed with introductions to Chinese officials, artists, and scholars, I was at last able to revisit Peking after an absence of thirty-two years. The Chinese authorities appeared to welcome me, possibly because they were intrigued by how or even why I operate my school, but more likely because I was paying a huge amount of money for a car and driver and a room in the Peking Hotel.

It would have been appropriate to return with Aimee, but we had been long separated. After reaching New York in 1951, Aimee took courses in chemistry at Columbia University, while I taught the history of Chinese art as best as I could at the old Asia Institute. Aimee's teachers lost no time in informing her that she was a roaring genius with a gift for abstract thought. My own position was less fortunate, it having been impressed upon me that I was something of an outcast in my own country thanks to a recently risen phenomenon called McCarthyism. According to these zealous patriots I had done the unforgivable by living, of my own free will, for two years in a Communist country. In the meantime, the Asia Institute was about to close and new job offers were scarce, particularly in light of my unsavory past, whereas Aimee, a refugee from communism, endowed with ambition and an exceptional brain, found opportunity waiting. Moreover, she had her share of the family jewelry and could sell a piece or two should the need arise.

We agreed that I should journey on to Japan, which would have been my destination anyway had not, understandably enough, Aimee so disliked the Japanese. After all, America had been her destination, and in America she should stay. We imagined then that we might one day be able to make a life together, but as the years passed and we developed new interests and pursued widely different careers, that possibility faded. Still, neither of us has remarried, and it pleases us both that we have remained friends to this day.

When I suggested that she join me in revisiting Peking, Aimee answered that she was too busy and would suffer too much at the sight of what had happened to China. Instead, she sent me Second Brother's latest address. He had been a judge, and I remembered him as a slightly deaf, proud-looking man of medium height in his early forties. Aimee had almost brought about his ruin some ten years earlier when she sent him a hearing aid from America. The Chinese postal authorities turned the package over to the police, who immediately identified its contents as an American spying device. I hoped he would be glad to see me.

Old China-hands, especially those who had already revisited China, were writing me from Bangkok, Hong Kong, and London to warn me not to return, saying that the Peking I knew had changed beyond all recognition. "It is no longer the 'city of lingering splendor' you remember. Its walls and gates have been destroyed, its temples have been turned into factories and schools." I knew all this, but like the passerby at the scene of the accident, I had to see for myself.

As my Chinese driver ferried me into Peking from the airport in our little Russian Volga, I looked out at the passing fields. The countryside seemed different. It took me some time to realize that the graves and tomb enclosures that had formerly dotted the fields were gone. If the dead were still there beneath the soil, all evidence of their existence had been erased. Passing through suburbs of new four- and five-story

169

gray brick buildings, I waited for the first glimpse of the old city. I knew the Communist government had destroyed the walls of Peking along with those of most cities throughout China as useless feudal relics, but I asked the driver to point out the spot where the old moats and walls had stood. Suddenly we were there, crossing above a sunken six-lane highway built where the moat had been. I expected to feel a pang, but when I looked down at the oddly empty highway and the blocks of ugly new buildings, where the walls had stood, stretching north and south along the perimeter of what had been the most fabled walled city in the world, I experienced for the first time the anger that would save me from despair during the days to come.

Old buildings began to appear, shabby and run-down. The gold and red shop signs so characteristic of Peking were gone, and the lacquered carvings on gates and buildings had been covered in gray plaster, as if camouflaged. Crowding the streets, people were dressed in the same shades of gray and seemed, like the carvings, to be avoiding attention. Even the resonant blue sky over Peking had turned gray-white—the result of pollution, my driver told me.

That evening I ate in the hotel dining room. The food was poor, most of the dishes being mounds of indistinguishable meats cooked in brown sauce, but I recognized them for what they would have been in the old days—a feast for peasants. This meal was characteristic of most of the food I was to eat in Peking during the next two weeks.

The sky was still light after sundown, and we set out on my first goal: to find the old Yu mansion on Crooked Hair Family Lane. My spoken Chinese, after decades of disuse, apparently worked since my driver pulled up some twenty minutes later in front of what should have been the entrance to the Yu mansion. I knew that the house had been converted in the 1960s from a clinic into the official residence of Lin Piao, the heir-designate to Mao Tse-tung, and that, after his mysterious death in an airplane crash over Mongolia, it had been opened to the public, eager to view the site of such high treason. But the Yu mansion was gone. Soldiers with bayonets stood guard beside a gate I had never seen before, while within, where the courtyards and gardens should have been, rose a forbidding, multistoried brick building—a branch office of the secret police, the driver said, warning me not to get out of the car. I did not. Nor was there anything I could say on the way back to the hotel. How could I explain to the young driver how much had been lost?

The next morning we set out again, this time to find Second Brother and the Yu family. My driver had informed the neighborhood police that I was coming, a necessary procedure at that time when a foreigner visited a Chinese. Stopping at a tumbledown door on a back lane, my driver stepped out to collide with a small, bespectacled, hunchbacked man rushing out of the door. The man looked puzzled. He didn't know any foreigners, he said excitedly, or why one was coming to see him. I thought we had found the wrong Yu, until I noticed a pink plastic hearing aid protruding from one of his ears. Getting out of the car myself, I shouted at him in Chinese "Don't you have a sister living in America?" He nodded, fiddling with the volume control inside his shirt pocket. "And didn't she marry an American?" He nodded again. "I am that American who married your sister." His face brightened. "Oh," he said in English, "Mr. Kitty."

By this time, a crowd of people emerging from the nearby houses had gathered around us, interested in the car and a Chinese-speaking foreigner. Second Brother quickly led me through the door into what once must have been a back kitchenyard, containing three small run-down buildings.

This cramped yard housed not only my brother-in-law's family, consisting of a wife and two grown sons, but four other families as well, whose various members now gaped at me as I followed Second Brother to his two rooms in the rear. Photographs showed me later that the floors of these rooms were of worn tile, but at the time, amid the smell of age and decay, I thought them earthen. The rooms were so small that I had to sit on a bed while I spoke mostly with Second Brother's son, who kindly yelled my questions at his father. Amid the jumble of stacked objects in the rooms, I identified from the old mansion a red lacquered trunk, a round, yellow pearwood table, which had stood in the Hall of Ancient Pines, and a celadon vase in which a feather duster now reposed.

Our conversation revealed that Second Brother had not been employed since 1956, when he had been sentenced to ten years of heavy labor. The government had called it "re-education." The rocks he had carried daily on his back eventually crushed his spine, leaving him the hunchbacked man I was looking at now. His wife was away teaching school. His eldest son was at work in a factory. Elder Brother worked in Tientsin and First Sister was dead. I knew that Aunt Chin had died years ago, before the brutalities of the Cultural Revolution. But I had not heard until now that her mute companion had cried soundlessly through the funeral, lay down on the last day and died herself, everyone agreed, of a heart broken beyond repair.

The hearing aid Second Brother wore was Chinese in manufacture and not very good, he said, Aimee's having been kept by the police. In 1966 his family had been evicted from the house I had seen them settled in before our departure by an officer of the Chinese army, although Fifth Sister and Ninth Sister were allowed to continue living in one of its rooms.

Second Brother's son was next dispatched to bring Fifth Sister. She would be over seventy now, and I almost dreaded seeing her, but when she entered the room I recognized her easily. Her short hair was still mostly black but, rather than the silk gowns of yore, she wore a much-washed white shirt, dark pants, and sandals.

Fifth Sister's hearing was fine and I was able to ask her directly about the Cultural Revolution and whether the family had suffered or not. She told me about the August massacre fifteen years earlier that, simultaneously in other cities through China, marked the beginning of the Cultural Revolution. By some miracle, the Yu family had survived, primarily, Fifth Sister told me, because no one had ever associated them with the Yu family that had lived in the great mansion in the West city.

Fifth Sister went on to tell me about the massacre of the residents of old Peking. The slaughter even had a name, Hung Pa Yueh—Bloody August. I was amazed that it had never been reported in the West, and said so to her. "The government wouldn't like it," Fifth Sister said.

Through the heat of that Bloody August, she told me, the young Red Guards had murdered the gentle citizens of old Peking. At night, the screams of the beaten and dying made sleep impossible. Almost anything, even owning the photograph of a grandfather, could be cause for being beaten to death. Rather than guns or knives, the Red Guards wielded clubs and sticks, prolonging the agony as they wished, striking to kill on the third blow or postponing the moment of death ten or fifteen minutes. It was said that as many as half a million people had died. She spoke of people covered with blood, women dragged by their hair through the streets, others hanging from trees, or drowned in Peking's lakes and moats. By the end of that month the dead were piled so high that they could not be burned fast enough in the huge new crematorium to the west that, then as today, is the last destination of all those who live and die in Peking.

We carried stools into the courtyard where my driver posed us for a photograph. In it, I am holding a palm fan lent me to stir the humid, unmoving air. Fifth Sister perches on an overturned pail while, seated on a stool, Second Brother smiles dispiritedly, showing broken teeth. Rags, frayed socks, and a faded pink undershirt hang on lines to our right and left. A washboard, part of an old bicycle, and pots and pans complete the picture. We all look like the laundry—limp and old. Called "useless people" in the New China, it seemed that no trace of my relatives' aristocratic past had survived.

Still, I could not forget that my presence here might embarrass or even endanger them, however fallen they might be, but when I invited them to dinner at the Peking Hotel, half-prepared for a polite refusal, they accepted without hesitation.

At the appointed time, I descended to the hotel lobby to find Fifth Sister, Ninth Sister, Second Brother, his wife, and two sons gathered around a desk at the entry, humbly writing down their names and addresses, a formality not required by those wearing party uniforms, fresh shirts, or even suits. Nothing I said enabled me to bring quickly to an end this humiliation to my family. I thought it ironic that, before the revolution, the Yu family had, on more than one occasion, rented the grand ballroom of the old Peking Hotel merely to entertain their friends.

I had arranged for a private room in the west wing which the waiters told me Chou En-lai had especially liked. It possessed a wainscoting of dark, shellacked wood, a sitting area with sofas and overstuffed chairs where we were first served tea and cigarettes, and a big round table where we ate. The conversation moved along easily, mostly about what had happened to people and, of course, what I knew about Aimee and her career as a physicist in America. I tried to explain her research on the aerodynamics of the tear drop shape, but only confused them. I had better luck explaining her involvement with NASA's Star Computer, which had put America's first space shuttle into orbit. Had my Chinese been better, her relatives might have been prouder of her achievements.

I quickly discovered in Peking that no one, including my relatives, liked to talk about their own misfortune. The stories of suffering I heard were usually told to me about other people. Eugene Chiang, for example, who wore the pink business suit at our garden party, had tried to cross into Hong Kong, they told me. He had been caught by the British and turned back to the Chinese, who clapped him in jail where he had sickened and died in less than a year.

Magdelene Grant's was a happier story. She had been seen last on the platform of the Peking railway station in 1954, carrying matched luggage and wearing a suit of white pongee silk, destination Singapore. No one has heard from her since.

My Chinese relatives were the first to tell me what I later discovered was a popular story in Peking about two American pilots who had been shot down during the Korean War. Captured and sent to solitary confinement in China, one died quickly, but the other knew Morse code and for twenty years tapped out on his cell wall the message. "I am an American. Help." By some miracle, a Chinese who knew both English and Morse code briefly occupied the adjoining cell, after which the story of the imprisoned American spread, eventually reaching Peking and Richard Nixon, there on his first visit, who effected the pilot's release. Whether true or not, the Chinese liked this story, I imagine, because it symbolized the blind circumstances of their own lives and the hope that kept them alive.

The food that evening was better than in the main dining room and should have been since it was about a hundred times more expensive. Fifth Sister asked me what the meal had cost and was astounded at the answer. "What a waste," she said, "that you have spent so much money on us," and meant it.

There was a sadness about my in-laws and their self-effacing behavior that I had never seen before, as if the New

China had beaten them down and kept them down so long that they had forgotten who they had been.

During the following days I was grateful that Peking's grander monuments still survived, but found visits to them painful. They were for me, like everything else in Peking, double exposures. I saw them as they had been thirty years ago, quiet and almost empty, their lacquered pillars and woodwork mellowed to pale turquoise and cinnabar, and I saw them now as cheaply repainted backdrops for hordes of misplaced sightseers from the provinces. Not a terrace, a corridor, or a flight of marble stairs was ever clear of them.

Only within the walls of the imperial Forbidden City could I imagine that the city surrounding it was unchanged. Although China's new rulers had once seriously considered dismantling the palace and replacing it with modern government office buildings as a more fitting heart to the New China, it still stands, thanks to their indulgence. The memories of emperors and gods have been moved aside, however, to house the people's museums, souvenir shops, curio stores, public toilets, and, for foreigners only, Coca-Cola vending machines.

From the Forbidden City's Gate of Heavenly Peace in the south to its northernmost gate is a walk of a mile or so, and I was overwhelmed, as of old, by its oceanic majesty and the illusion it created of supernatural space and time. As I walked, the repetition and variation of architectural themes—the red-walled and yellow-roofed buildings on marble terraces one behind the other—moved slowly past me like huge gold and crimson waves.

On another day I found the Altar of Heaven, a three-tiered disk of white marble, built on the sacred multiples of threes and nines, blazing in the sunlight. A group of American tourists were there, playing hopscotch on the flagstones, their goal the central disk where once only China's emperors had knelt to worship heaven. The watching Chinese appeared to take the whole thing with good humor. In the old days they would have been less pleased, still aware that this place, though no longer in use, was sacred to China.

In the lanes where Peking's old mansions still stood, large gateways signified once-great houses within, but jerry-built shacks, sheds, and lean-tos obliterated their lines. Inside, the courtyards and former gardens were filled with still more shacks and sheds to house the millions of children born over the last thirty years who, grown and married themselves, live in these vestiges of privacy.

Nothing old, except those palaces or temples open to tourists, had been repaired since I left, as if by policy— "Forget the old. Build the new." Nor were persons and objects where they had been thirty years before. Everything and everyone seemed not only to have moved, but to have moved often.

My time in Peking was growing short and I had yet to visit my old residence at the Summer Palace. Despite a dark sky and predictions of rain, my driver and I headed out of the city. On the way, we would pass the former Yenching University campus and the home of my old friend and colleague, Bob Winter. At the age of ninety-six, he was my oldest living friend. A student of Ezra Pound, Bob had come to Peking in the twenties and stayed to collect Ming furniture and breed rare strains of iris. He had lived so long in China that, after the Communist take-over, he chose to stay.

After some searching, my driver found Bob's little house. Meeting me at the door, he was old but identifiably himself and still spoke the same careful, precise English I remembered so well. He greeted me warmly, and I reminded him of the years during which we had been friends. He nodded. "Of course I remember you," he said, and led me to a small bed-room where I took a chair while he propped himself up on his bed. To my surprise, I recognized a fifteenth-century Ming table next to the bed which Bob had always owned, and opened up, I knew, into a game board.

I had already heard that Bob had been chained to his bed for six months toward the end of the Cultural Revolution and wanted to ask if it had been to this bed. "Bob," I said instead, "tell me about the Red Guards." I wasn't sure he would be willing to talk about them, but he suddenly sat straight up. "Those snotty-nosed high school students," he said. "They hated everything old." Released from school in 1966, stu-dents throughout China had gone wild destroying art, books, and people. By the end of the Cultural Revolution in 1975, Bob told me, they and their successors had come to believe that anyone born in pre-Communist China was beyond re-educating and should simply be eliminated.

Bob told me about the Dance of Loyalty, which every Chinese had to be able to perform to prove his faith in Mao. The Ministry of Culture had created this dance and the song that accompanied it. The unfortunate performer was required to hop first on one foot and then on the other, while singing the oath of loyalty before a portrait of Mao Tse-tung. Bob swung his arms. At the end of the song the performer bowed deeply to the portrait while holding Mao's little red book over his head in both hands. A beating, prison, or even death was meted out to those, however old and lame, who could not perform this dance or remember the words to the song.

In effect, the young had been turned loose upon the old. All other tyrannies pale by comparison. "I am a student of history," Bob continued. "Nothing like this ever happened before anywhere in the world."

I better understood now the life-weary expressions I had seen as often on the faces of the young as on the old. Without a glance at the Volga, bicyclists and pedestrians would swerve into its path. Maneuvering around them, my driver would say, "Chinese aren't afraid to die. It's easy to die, but hard to live."

It began to rain as Bob talked on about his memories of China, his illnesses, his puzzling longevity, and the stern aunts who had raised him in Iowa almost a century earlier.

Later, standing in the doorway to say good-bye, he appeared so ancient I wondered that he could still be alive. He looked beyond me into the falling rain before he took my hand, squeezed it, and asked, "Who were you? Did I know you well?"

At the Summer Palace, it was still raining and the crowds of damp people filling the long galleries were more than I could bear. I stopped in a lakeside pavilion and sat on a re-painted balustrade looking out at the gray rain-flattened lake. Its level had sunk several feet, leaving the marble piers, where our barges and boats had once moored, high in mud. This lake and all the ornamental lakes and moats of Peking had been fed by a spring of clear water originating at the Jade Fountain a few miles to the west of the Summer Palace. But the new factories built in and around Peking had not only polluted the air, but had used up the underground water. The Jade Fountain had gone dry, while the muddy river water that now served Peking's needs was not even enough to fill the lake.

Too much rain and too many people kept me from climbing the Mountain of Ten Thousand years up to the Sea of Wisdom at its summit. Instead, I made my way back to the east entrance and drove to the North Gate where there would be fewer people and a rear path I remembered that also led up to the Sea of Wisdom. But first, I would have to pass through my gate.

Externally it was unchanged and, to my surprise, the

stairway leading to its upper floor was unbarred. When the gatekeeper looked away I quickly climbed it. No one stopped me on the balcony either, and I slipped through the open doors into my old rooms. Rusty tools, cans of paint, and broken glass filled the spaces between some ten to fifteen straw-covered trestle beds, while lines of gray laundry hung criss-crossed between the pillars. The silk paintings in the high transoms between the rooms were in tatters, as was the once-translucent paper on the latticed windows that the director had put up for me more than thirty years earlier.

Back at the bottom of the stairs I looked from the shelter of the gate into the sodden palace grounds and the thin film of mud covering the marble bridge that I had to cross to reach the path leading up the hill. On impulse, I asked the gate-keeper if the Sea of Wisdom was open. It was closed, she said. I inquired about the Buddhas. "Three big old Buddhas?" she asked. "Yes," I answered, "three big old Buddhas." "Ah," she said, "They were destroyed by the Red Guards more than ten years ago." She must have felt that she had already told more to a foreigner than she should and would say no more, except that the Sea of Wisdom was closed because there was nothing inside to see.

I stood there trying to imagine the frenzied Red Guards toppling those huge statues, smashing them to pieces, and carting the pieces away—to be made, I supposed, into useful objects, like the truckloads of bronze images stripped from Tibet's temples that were melted down daily, a friend of mine who had once lived on the Sino-Tibetan border told me, to make ammunition.

I should have been grateful to the Red Guards. They had saved me a long climb in the rain. That night I lay awake try-ing to make sense of all I had seen.

Returning to Peking had been like stepping into the vortex of a storm. For me, China was still a grand stage on which all action took place in sharp contrasts. Everything was exaggerated and brutally real. Perhaps the contrasts I found were not just between poverty and wealth, wisdom and stupidity, beauty and ugliness, sanity and madness, but at some elemental level were contrasts between life and death.

Here in Peking I had the feeling that I had seen life more clearly and death more clearly, whereas in the indulgent world of the West, with its illusion of continuity and safety, outlines were blurred, concealing the rude truth: that life for us, as for them, is short, and that the struggle to preserve human dignity never ceases. On these profound thoughts, combined with a sedative, I finally fell asleep.

Two days before I was to leave Peking, Second Brother's son visited me at the hotel. He was smaller than his ancestors and, although his face was sweet, it was pale and pinched, the result, I imagined, of malnutrition in childhood. He delivered a letter to me from his father. Although Second Brother had written it in pencil, on lined notebook paper, it was, nevertheless, a formal invitation in the classical language, expressing his unworthiness to hold a farewell family dinner in my honor at Fifth Sister's the following night, my last night in Peking. I had not expected so much hospitality, but despite the danger it might cause the family, since neighbors would talk and the local police would have to be informed again, I gladly accepted.

The next afternoon, I bought Western cigarettes and soap in the hotel, imagining that they might be useful luxuries unobtainable by my family. I was later to be especially thankful that I also bought a bagful of English hard candies.

Second Brother and Fifth Sister were waiting at the curb before the address on Ch'ang-an Avenue I had been given. They led me down a dark alleyway to the house. As I entered the courtyard, the army officer's wife and children, squatting around a wooden tub, eyed me suspiciously. Nothing had been painted or repaired since I had last been there. Laundry on lines, primitive cooking stoves, and piles of rubble filled the place. Passing through a little kitchen, which I remembered as a vestibule, we entered a room containing a cupboard, two iron cots on which the bedding was neatly folded, an old foot-operated sewing machine, a portrait of Chou En-lai on the wall, some plain metal chairs, and two folding tables pushed together where we were to dine. I had slept in this room just before leaving China. Then it had been carpeted and filled with rosewood cabinets, bronzes, porcelains, and paintings from the old mansion.

The furniture, they told me, had been sold to government buying offices by weight (antiques and art could be sold only to the government), while the five-hundred-year-old bronze incense burners, doused long ago by Little Blackie, had also been sold by weight and melted down like the Buddhas to make objects of greater use to New China.

Some twenty members of the Yu family, including children and grandchildren I had never seen before, were gathered to greet me. Together we ate the food that they had prepared—as close to a feast of old as was possible in the New China. There were four kinds of *chiao-tze* (meat and vegetables wrapped in pastry and steamed), chicken, diced pork with fried peanuts (a dish they remembered I had liked), almond soup, and much more.

At the end of the meal, the grandchildren, who had eaten outside, were brought in to be formally presented. One by one, each child came before me, bowed, and called out, "Grandfather!" To be sure, this was the title by which they should have addressed me, but it had never occurred to me that I was so old or that youngsters I did not even know would regard me as a family elder. Like an aged patriarch, I would like to have presented each of them with a gold sovereign, but gave them instead the bag of English candies.

The Dunhill cigarettes and the cakes of lavender soap I

gave to their parents, who thanked me. They still lay untouched on the table illuminated by a bare overhead bulb when the room suddenly fell silent as Ninth Sister entered carrying a large box in her hands.

"This is for you," she said, putting it in front of me on the table. "It's nothing special."

The family watched as I lifted the lid to discover inside a pair of brand-new cloisonné vases costing for them, I had no doubt, a month's wages. Instantly the cigarettes and soap seemed close to insult. How could I repay them or, for that matter, make them understand without appearing ungrateful that they shouldn't have made so huge a sacrifice for me? And then I saw them smiling at my discomfiture, and it was I who understood. They were reminding me that they were still the Yu family, people of culture to whom the old ways still mattered, and that they were honored that I had come to visit them after so many years and from so far away. I picked one up to find that its motif, executed in white, brown, and pink enamel, was plum blossoms in snow symbolizing, as it always had in Chinese art, the rugged ability to survive adversity. I accepted the vases with gratitude and a sudden lightening of the heart as the family looked on approvingly.

Later, waving farewell at the curbside as the car pulled away, the boxed vases safely on the seat beside me, Second Brother and Fifth Sister looked proud and even a little bold, the way I remembered they had looked in years long gone by.

ABOUT THE TYPE

The text of this book has been set in Trump Mediaeval. Designed by Georg Trump for the Weber foundry in the late 1950s, this typeface is a modern rethinking of the Garalde Oldstyle types (often associated with Claude Garamond) that have long been popular with printers and book designers.

Trump Mediaeval is a trademark of
Linotype-Hell AG and/or its subsidiaries

TITLES IN SERIES